Evaluation of Delaware's Opportunity Funding and Student Success Block Grant Programs

Early Implementation

SY DOAN, HEATHER L. SCHWARTZ, DANIELLA HENRY, LYNN A. KAROLY

Sponsored by the Delaware Department of Education

RAND EDUCATION AND LABOR

For more information on this publication, visit www.rand.org/t/RRA230-1

Library of Congress Cataloging-in-Publication Data is available for this publication.
ISBN: 978-1-9774-0634-7

Published by the RAND Corporation, Santa Monica, Calif.

Preface

This report is the first of three annual reports evaluating the implementation and effects of two Delaware weighted funding programs for disadvantaged schools during the 2019–2020 to 2021–2022 school years. The Opportunity Fund, which, in 2019–2020, was a newly expanded version of a pilot program in the state, is the first funding program. The second is the Student Success Block Grant (SSBG) program—in its second year as of the 2019–2020 school year.

The authors of this report examine the implementation of both programs and emerging best practices from the Opportunity Fund and the SSBG in 2019–2020, as reported by local education agency (LEA) leaders. (The school year 2019–2020 corresponds to fiscal year 2020.) More specifically, we examine how LEAs planned to use the funds and how they were actually used; expenditures under the funding mechanisms; and LEA leaders' reported barriers to implementation of their plans and best practices for serving English learner (EL), low-income (LI), and special education students. Because state testing was canceled in spring 2020 because of COVID-19, we only examine spending and implementation and not student outcomes as originally intended. In light of the pandemic, we also report how LEAs modified their Opportunity Fund and SSBG investments. The study is funded through a contract with the Delaware Department of Education (DDOE) to conduct an independent evaluation of these two funding mechanisms.

The state legislature allocated $25 million in Opportunity Fund for fiscal year 2020 to give school districts supplemental funding for LI and EL students, as well as for mental health programming at elementary schools serving disadvantaged students. The SSBG program allocated almost $4.5 million in fiscal year 2020 for disadvantaged schools to hire reading interventionists, as well as almost $4 million for special education programming in grades K–3.

The report will be of interest to Delaware state-level policymakers in the executive and legislative branches, including DDOE and legislative staff, as well as other stakeholders in the public and private sectors interested in the potential for strategic investments in the early elementary grades to improve student outcomes. The findings for Delaware should be of interest to policymakers in other parts of the United States considering or making similar investments.

This study was undertaken by RAND Education and Labor, a division of the RAND Corporation that conducts research on early childhood through postsecondary education programs, workforce development, and programs and policies affecting workers, entrepreneurship, and financial literacy and decisionmaking. This study was sponsored by the DDOE.

More information about RAND can be found at www.rand.org. Questions about this report should be directed to Sy Doan (qdoan@rand.org), and questions about RAND Education and Labor should be directed to educationandlabor@rand.org.

Contents

Figures

Tables

Summary

In 2019, Delaware created a weighted student funding system, whereby the Delaware Department of Education (DDOE) provides supplemental funds to school districts on the basis of enrollment of low income (LI), English learner (EL), and elementary-grade special education (SPED) students. The additional funding was in recognition of the longstanding gaps in achievement between these student subgroups and students overall in Delaware, as is the case nationally.

To assess the effectiveness of the new funding, the legislature also required an independent evaluation of the programs. As the independent evaluator, the RAND Corporation is evaluating Delaware's Opportunity Fund and Student Success Block Grant (SSBG) programs for the three-year period of 2019–2020 through 2021–2022. The Opportunity Fund provides two streams of financial support to schools—one that is flexible for local education agencies (LEAs) to fund staff, curriculum, or services that serve LI and EL students and a second for either mental health supports or reading supports for high-need schools. The SSBG also has two streams of financial support for schools—one that offers additional funding to LEAs based on the number of K–3 basic SPED enrollees and a second that covers the hiring of one reading interventionist in each high-need elementary school. The Delaware legislature allocated a total of $33.5 million for both the Opportunity Fund and SSBG programs, of which districts expended $25.9 million in 2019–2020.

In this first of three annual reports, in addition to a final best-practices guide, we analyzed proposed versus actual investments that LEAs and schools made with the Opportunity Fund and SSBG dollars in the 2019–2020 school year; LEA expenditures within each funding stream; LEA leaders' perceived barriers and best investments to aid EL, LI, and SPED students; and adjustments to these investments they made because of COVID-19. We performed our analysis by coding and summarizing LEA expenditures, surveys of superintendents and SSBG reading interventionists, and LEAs' applications and updates about their use of Opportunity Fund and SSBG monies.

Our key findings include:

- Participation in both Opportunity Fund and SSBG programs was high. Forty out of 41 of Delaware's LEAs applied for and received flexible Opportunity Fund monies. Meanwhile, 27 LEAs expended one or both types of SSBG funds, which were targeted to elementary-grade schools for SPED and to provide a reading interventionist in schools with high percentages of LI or EL students.

- Although initial allocations for the flexible Opportunity Fund and SSBG K–3 basic SPED funding programs were made equitably on a per-pupil basis, the actual fiscal year (FY) 2020 per-pupil amounts that LEAs expended differed substantially based on which investments LEAs made, how much of their allocation they left unspent, and differences across LEAs in pay scale and experience levels for staff hires. Flexible Opportunity Fund per-pupil expenditures ranged from $141 to $514 per disadvantaged student, and SSBG K–3 basic SPED funding expenditures ranged from $147 to $1,118 per K–3 SPED student.
- By far, the most frequent proposed use of both Opportunity Fund and SSBG monies was to hire new staff. A little more than half of the LEAs' 185 combined proposed investments with Opportunity Fund flexible monies were for new staff, compared with 27 professional development (PD) investments, the next most frequent type of investment. The most common staff positions were in-school mental health staff (e.g., counselors, social workers, psychologists), English as a second language (ESL)–certified teachers, and reading interventionists. The next most common uses of the funds were for teacher PD and student curriculum materials.
- As of April 2020, LEAs reported that 71 percent of their 185 total proposed flexible Opportunity Fund investments were fully implemented. They were most likely to fully implement hires of new staff and least likely to fully implement new student programming, such as summer programming (very possibly because of COVID-19). Roughly 60 percent of LEAs reported encountering barriers to implementing at least one of their flexible Opportunity Fund investments.
- LEAs left 30 percent of Opportunity Fund FY 2020 mental health allocations unspent by the end of the year. This was the highest percentage of unspent funds across the four funding streams we examined. Shortages of certified staff may be one reason; social workers and psychologists are the two job categories for which virtually all Delaware certificated individuals are already employed in Delaware public schools.
- The Opportunity Fund mental health program had greater inequality in allocated funding across qualifying schools because LEA applications, rather than per pupil allocations, drove the per-school allocated amounts. In the 44 applications for mental health funding, LEAs requested as few as one to as many as six investments per qualifying school, with amounts ranging from $46,956 to $257,784.
- In general, charter school LEAs spent down their flexible Opportunity Funds and SSBG K–3 allocations more fully than did traditional public school districts.
- New staff, followed by additional PD, were the first- and second-ranked investments that most LEA leaders identified as the most effective for promoting improved academic outcomes among LI, EL, and SPED students. Additional programming and supplies were among the least-mentioned types of investments they perceived as being most effective.

- Despite COVID-19, most LEAs continued to use their Opportunity Fund and SSBG investments during spring 2020, modifying some staff roles to better serve students and families via remote learning.

Given that the majority of Opportunity Fund and SSBG investments are directed toward hiring new staff, particularly for staff with skills and certification with regard to English language learners and student mental health, LEAs' ability to recruit, hire, and compensate staff with these credentials should be closely examined as a key factor of whether they are able to spend out their allocations. Delaware certification programs should seek to expand recruitment of candidates for social workers, school psychologists, and other shorthanded roles because LEA leaders are likely to continue focusing on providing mental health and social and emotional learning services in the wake of COVID-19.

Acknowledgments

The authors thank the Delaware Department of Education staff for the extremely helpful support for and participation in the study. We especially thank Susan Bunting, Delaware Secretary of Education, and her staff, including Susan Haberstroh, Kathy Kelly, Kimberly Klein, Zubaca Nermin, and Adrian Peoples. They have responded promptly and fully to our requests for data and information and greatly aided the evaluation.

This report benefited substantively from quality assurance feedback from Fatih Unlu, a RAND Education and Labor quality assurance manager. We also thank our two reviewers, Elizabeth Steiner and Henry Tran, who helped us improve the clarity and completeness of the report.

Abbreviations

DDOE	Delaware Department of Education
EL	English learner
ESL	English as a second language
FTE	full-time equivalent
FY	fiscal year
LEA	local education agency
LI	low income
PBIS	Positive Behavior and Intervention Supports
PD	professional development
SEL	social and emotional learning
SPED	special education
SSBG	Student Success Block Grant
SWD	students with disabilities

1. Introduction

A little more than one-quarter of Delaware public school students in 2019–2020 come from low-income (LI) families, and one-tenth are English learners (ELs). In recognition of achievement gaps between LI and EL students and the rest of the Delaware student population, Governor John Carney introduced a weighted pupil funding system for Delaware in 2019. In addition to the state's traditional unit-based funding, the state legislature allocated funding for disadvantaged students via the expansion of two funding initiatives: the Opportunity Fund and the Student Success Block Grant (SSBG).

Through the Opportunity Fund, the Delaware Department of Education (DDOE) awards grants annually to local education agencies (LEAs) for additional funding on the basis of LI and EL student enrollment to direct toward investments designed to improve academic performance specifically for these students. The Opportunity Fund, which started in smaller form in 2017–2018 and expanded by 2019–2020, increases supports for LI and EL students through two mechanisms. First, per-pupil flexible funds are allocated to LEAs—$500 per LI student and $300 per EL student—to pay for staff, curriculum, or other services that the LEAs identify as most needed to serve their LI and EL students, subject to state approval based on a written plan. Beginning in 2019–2020, these supports started at $20 million each year over three years. But a recent legal settlement in October 2020 will render the program permanent, with a significant increase in funding to $60 million per year by 2025. Second, Opportunity Fund dollars fund mental health services in *high-need elementary schools*, defined as schools with student enrollments made up of at least 60 percent LI students and/or 20 percent EL students. The state of Delaware will allocate a total of $15 million for these mental health–related supports over the three years of 2019–2020 to 2021–2022.

The SSBG program started in the 2018–2019 school year and was funded at $8.5 million in 2019–2020. Similar to the Opportunity Fund, the SSBG has two funding components: (1) formula grants for LEAs based on the number of K–3 basic special education (SPED) enrollees to fund additional SPED services and (2) grants for high-need elementary schools to hire a reading interventionist for the academic year (ten months).

All of Delaware's 16 traditional public school districts, three vocational-technical districts, and 22 charter school networks are eligible, and all but one applied for and received Opportunity Funds. We refer to these 41 districts and charter school networks collectively as LEAs throughout the report. In 2019–2020, 40 of the 41 LEAs received Opportunity Fund flexible monies, 15 received Opportunity Fund mental health supports, 27 received SSBG SPED funds, and 15 received SSBG funds for a reading interventionist.

The DDOE contracted with the RAND Corporation to conduct an independent evaluation over three years to understand how LEAs use the Opportunity Funds and SSBG and whether the two initiatives are having their intended favorable effects on LI, EL, and SPED students. This report is the first of three annual reports that document the three-year evaluation of these programs, as shown in Table 1.1.

Assessing the performance of the Opportunity Fund and SSBG programs in the first year has been complicated by the extraordinary circumstances of the COVID-19 pandemic starting in spring 2020. The governor announced the closure of Delaware public schools, effective March 16, 2020. Like districts nationally, LEAs in the state turned to remote learning, with some offering offline instructional materials, given a lack of universal broadband access and internet-connected devices at home. Other LEAs eventually shifted to all-online instruction. Delaware public schools remained in remote instruction for the rest of the 2019–2020 school year. Additionally, like other states, the DDOE canceled spring statewide standardized student assessments. Thus, although this first-year evaluation report cannot assess any program impacts on student outcomes during the 2019–2020 school year, it considers the consequences of pandemic disruptions for the deployment of resources supported by the Opportunity Fund and SSBG.

Table 1.1. Overview of Planned Evaluation Reports

Year 1	Year 2	Year 3
• Literature review • LEAs' intended and actual activities using the Opportunity Fund and SSBG • LEA expenditures during year 1 • LEA leaders' perceived barriers to implementing planned use of funds • LEA leaders' perception of the most effective practices in use of funds • COVID-19 disruption and response	• LEAs' intended and actual activities using the Opportunity Fund and SSBG • LEA expenditures during year 2 and trends in expenditures • Interviews of LEA leaders • Analysis of effects of the Opportunity Fund and SSBG on student achievement	• LEAs' intended and actual activities using the Opportunity Fund and SSBG • LEA expenditures during year 3 and trends in expenditures • Interviews of LEA leaders • Analysis of effects of the Opportunity Fund and SSBG funds on student achievement • Three case studies of LEAs

Research Questions and Approach

The goal of this first evaluation report is to examine how Delaware's LEAs invested their Opportunity Fund and SSBG allocations during the 2019–2020 academic year, any barriers to implementation encountered by district and charter school leaders, and the best practices as identified by LEA leaders during the first year of the expanded Opportunity Fund and SSBG programs. Additionally, in light of the COVID-19 pandemic, we report on the efforts made by LEAs to continue or modify their investments during the transition to remote learning. More specifically, we examine the following research questions using a combination of document review, literature review, qualitative coding, and descriptive analysis:

1. What does existing research suggest is most effective for improving the outcomes of LI, EL, and SPED students?
2. How much Opportunity Fund and SSBG monies did LEAs expend?
3. What investments did they propose to make with their Opportunity Fund and SSBG resources during the 2019–2020 school year? How successful were LEAs in implementing what they originally proposed?
4. How did LEAs adapt their Opportunity Fund and SSBG investments for remote learning during the COVID-19 pandemic?
5. What did LEA leaders perceive as the most effective uses of the Opportunity Fund and SSBG during the 2019–2020 school year?

To address these questions, we draw on DDOE fiscal and administrative data about Opportunity Fund and SSBG implementation, LEAs' midyear and summative conference reports regarding progress with Opportunity Fund and SSBG implementation submitted to the DDOE, and results from a survey of LEAs that RAND administered in April 2020. Because of the cancellation of spring 2020 statewide student achievement tests following the pandemic-related cessation of in-person learning, we have not included an analysis of student achievement as originally intended. We do, however, anticipate including this analysis in the year 2 report and in the final year 3 report, as shown in Table 1.1.

We continue in Chapter 2 with more detail about the genesis and design of the Opportunity Fund and SSBG programs, as well as a review of relevant prior research. In Chapter 3, we describe the data and methods we used to answer the five research questions. In Chapter 4, we set out our findings. We offer our conclusions and a discussion of the implications of the results in Chapter 5.

2. Background: Local Education Agency Context, Funding Design, and Prior Literature

To set the context for the findings, this chapter provides an overview of the characteristics of Delaware students and districts and an overview of the Opportunity Fund and SSBG programs. We also summarize prior research on the efficacy of more school funding generally and targeted educational funding programs, including for student mental health, SPED, reading programs, and EL programming, areas of focus for the Opportunity Fund and SSBG.

Characteristics of Delaware LEAs

According to data obtained through the Delaware Open Data Portal, there are 16 traditional public school districts, three vocational-technical districts,[1] and 22 charter school networks in Delaware. These 41 LEAs served roughly 46,000 LI students and 15,000 EL students across the state during the 2019–2020 school year. LI and EL students comprise 31 and 10 percent, respectively, of the overall Delaware public school population. In Table A.1 in the Appendix, we list student enrollment and demographic characteristics for each of the 40 LEAs[2] included in our analysis. Among the 40 LEAs that participated in any of the four Opportunity Fund or SSBG funding components, overall per pupil expenditures in 2019–2020 ranged from a low of $10,248 per enrollee to a high of $28,256 per enrollee, inclusive of the four funding streams we examine (Table A.2). Put in context, the Opportunity Fund added as much as 5 percent to LEA overall spending, and the SSBG funding contributed as much as 2 percent.

Description of Delaware Educational Investment Programs

The Opportunity Fund, as of school year 2019–2020, was the third iteration of a state-specific program first piloted in 2017–2018, then known as Opportunity Grants. SSBG started in 2018–2019 and was in its second iteration during 2019–2020. The features of the two targeted funding programs since inception are listed in Table 2.1, which includes the unit at which funding was granted, grades and student subgroups of focus, and criteria by which funds were granted (i.e., through grant applications, on the basis of per-pupil enrollments, or on the basis of

---

[1] Three districts—Polytech, New Castle County, and Sussex Technical—house vocational-technical high schools. Polytech and Sussex Technical consist of a single vocational-technical high school, and New Castle County contains four vocational-technical high schools.

[2] The Delaware Military Academy is the 41st LEA that did not participate in any of the four funding programs.

meeting a "high-need" threshold set by the DDOE and defined as schools whose student enrollments are at least either 60 percent LI and/or 20 percent EL).

Table 2.1. Delaware Targeted Funding Programs: 2017–2018 to 2019–2020

Year	Program	Unit	Grades	Subgroup	Criteria
2017–2018	Opportunity Grants (nine schools)	School	K–12	LI, EL	Application
2018–2019	Opportunity Grants (threshold)	School	K–12	LI, EL	Threshold
2018–2019	SSBG: basic SPED	LEA	K–3	SPED	Per pupil
2018–2019	SSBG: reading interventionist	School	K–4	LI, EL	Threshold
2019–2020	Opportunity Fund: LI and EL flexible funding	LEA	K–12	LI, EL	Per pupil
2019–2020	Opportunity Fund: mental health/reading interventionist services	School	K–5	All	Threshold
2019–2020	SSBG: basic SPED	LEA	K–3	SPED	Per pupil
2019–2020	SSBG: reading interventionist	School	K–4	LI, EL	Threshold

The Opportunity Fund

The Delaware legislature appropriated a total of $25 million for the Opportunity Fund for the 2019–2020 year.[3] Any LEA with EL or LI enrollees or qualifying elementary schools was eligible to apply. The DDOE awarded Opportunity Funds to applicant LEAs on the basis of LI and EL district enrollments from the prior academic year in two streams:

1. flexible funding to enhance services for EL and LI students
2. school-based grants to fund mental health services and/or additional reading supports in high-need elementary schools, defined as schools that serve at least grades K–5 with student enrollments made up of at least 60 percent LI students and/or 20 percent EL students.

The flexible Opportunity Fund can cover all personnel costs, contracted services, supplies, materials, or other expenditures that the LEA proposed and DDOE approved in the LEA application. The funding can support hiring new staff for academic support, wraparound services, or mental health supports. The mental health funding, meanwhile, is more specifically used for "mental health services in the form of school counselors, school social workers or

[3] More specifically, the legislature appropriated $12.5 million in the operating budget and $37.5 million in a one-time supplemental bill (to be spent over three years). As a result of an October 2020 legal settlement, funding through the Opportunity Fund is set to increase to $60 million per year by 2024–2025 and became a permanent targeted education funding stream.

licensed clinical social workers, school psychologists, and/or for additional reading supports for grades K–5,"[4] as indicated in the LEA application form for this funding component.

To receive Opportunity Funds for the 2019–2020 academic year, LEAs must have submitted an application with expenditure plans to the DDOE by July 10, 2019.[5] Of the 41 LEAs in the state, 40 applied and were eventually approved for the flexible Opportunity Funds in 2019–2020. The DDOE approved each of the applications (with some modifications), and then set goals with LEA leaders at the beginning of the 2019–2020 school year, enacted a mid-year progress evaluation, and finally held a summative conference with each LEA leader in spring 2020.

The Opportunity Fund was a substantial expansion of the earlier Opportunity Grants program. In its first year, the Opportunity Grants program allocated $1 million to nine schools through a series of competitive sub-grants to provide specific student services targeting EL and LI students. Funding amounts were determined in accordance with the specific expenditures proposed by each school in its application. In its second year of operation (2018–2019), the Opportunity Grants program changed the manner in which it distributed funds in two ways that made it more similar to the current version of the Opportunity Fund program. First, Opportunity Grant *eligibility* was determined by enrollment thresholds of EL and LI students instead of through a competitive application process. Delaware schools whose enrollments were at least 60 percent LI and/or at least 20 percent EL were eligible to receive Opportunity Grants in 2018–2019. As a result, the number of schools receiving grants increased from nine in 2017–2018 to 46 in 2018–2019. Second, 2018–2019 Opportunity Grant *amounts* were determined based on the number of EL and LI pupils a school enrolled in the previous academic year.

A University of Delaware evaluation of 2018–2019 grantees' fall and mid-year self-reports found that the majority of grantees indicated using Opportunity Grant funds for integrated student supports (i.e., wraparound services, such as counselors, social and emotional learning [SEL] programming, and Sheltered Instruction Observation Protocol training and certification for teachers) and/or EL student supports, with test scores and disciplinary infractions being the most common metrics grantees used to evaluate themselves (Klein, Mead, and Shapiro, 2019). The authors note that more than 60 percent of grantees self-reported that they were "on track" to meet performance goals but provided no other evidence of program efficacy.

---

[4] This quote comes from the DDOE's application form for Opportunity Fund Mental Health program, dated September 2020. It is not publicly available.

[5] Prior to LEAs submitting applications, the DDOE notified each LEA of the total amount of flexible Opportunity Funds for which they qualified based on prior year EL and LI enrollments. This amount was calculated as follows: $300 * number of LI enrollees in 2018–2019 + $500 * number of EL enrollees in 2018–2019.

Student Success Block Grant

Delaware created the SSBG program, which was first implemented during the 2018–2019 school year, to distribute funding to better support students with disabilities, struggling readers, and student mental and emotional health via three mechanisms. Two of these have occurred in practice, but the third, which was $340,000 for school-based health and wellness centers in high-need elementary schools as directed by the Delaware Department of Health and Social Services, has not, and we do not include it in our analysis.

The two active SSBG distribution mechanisms are as follows:

1. The SSBG K–3 program provides additional funding for SPED in elementary schools. These are allocated on a formula basis; LEAs did not need to apply for the funds. The DDOE allocated funds to LEAs proportionately based on the number of grade K–3 students enrolled in the LEA who are eligible for basic SPED.[6] This mechanism provided LEAs $4.49 million in 2019–2020.
2. The SSBG reading program funds one ten-month reading interventionist per school in qualifying schools. The funding was available to all schools that served grades K–4 and had at least 60 percent LI and/or at least 20 percent EL students; this is the same eligibility criteria used by the 2018–2019 Opportunity Grants Program. Schools that qualified to receive these funds in 2018–2019 but no longer met the criteria in 2019–2020 were still able to receive the SSBG funds. And if funds were available, the DDOE could newly grant SSBG funding to schools who newly met the demographic criteria in 2019–2020. The SSBG reading program was funded at $3.97 million in 2019–2020 and the DDOE authorized and funded 45 total reading interventionist positions in eligible schools, which spanned 15 LEAs.

Delaware's Educator Workforce

During the 2019–2020 school year, a total of 19,046 full-time equivalent (FTE) staff were employed in Delaware K–12 public schools, 52 percent of whom were classroom teachers (see Figure 2.1). The number of classroom teachers has grown by 10 percent over the last five school years. Although the overall number of K–12 staff has generally grown, there was a decrease in staff who were not classified as classroom teachers from 2018–2019 to 2019–2020. As of the 2019–2020 school year, Delaware's classroom teachers were 83 percent white, 11 percent Black,

---

[6] Delaware uses three student SPED designations for the purposes of student funding: (1) basic, (2) intensive, and (3) complex. These designations, listed in order of intensity, differ according to required adult-student ratios, need for assistive technology, need for out-of-school or related services, and need for accommodations.

3 percent Hispanic/Latino, and 77 percent female. Eighteen percent of classroom teachers were described as "early career" teachers who are within the first four years of their careers.

Figure 2.1. Total Full-Time Equivalent Staff Working in Delaware Public Schools, 2015–2016 to 2019–2020

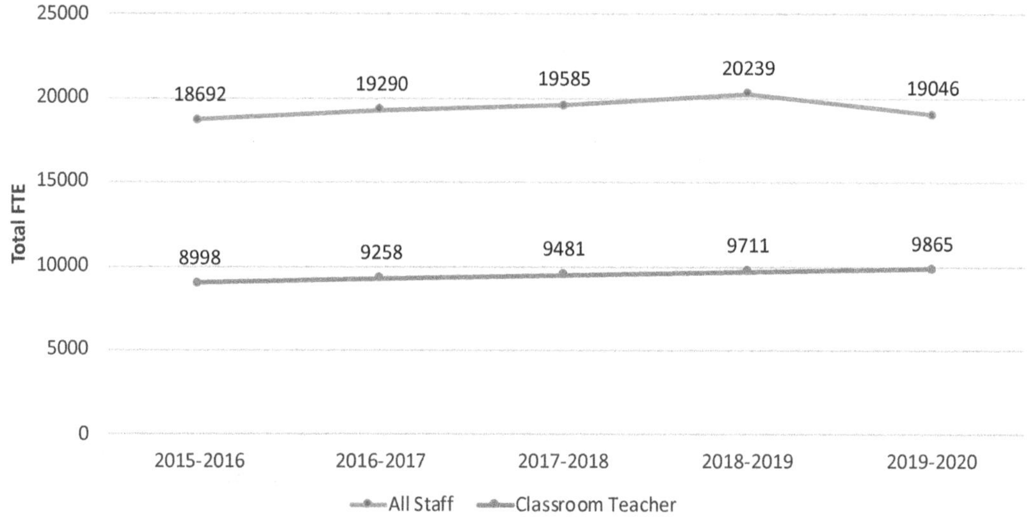

SOURCE: Delaware Open Data, 2020a.

Given that the Opportunity Fund and SSBG programs support hiring staff and providing services to better serve EL, LI, and SPED students, as well as increasing reading supports via reading interventionists, we also examine patterns in specific staff positions and their certification in the state. In Table 2.2 we present the total FTEs, by year, of staff who are (1) both employed and actively certified for a particular role in a given school year and (2) actively certified regardless of employment in a Delaware public school for that particular role in a given school year. Similar to the growth in classroom teachers overall (shown in Figure 2.1), the number of FTE staff in most categories presented in Table 2.2 grew over time. The exception was bilingual teachers, where both the number of total employed FTEs and certified employees decreased from 2015–2016 to 2019–2020.

Table 2.2. Number of Certificated and Employed Staff by Type, 2015–2016 to 2019–2020

Staff Type	Status	2015–2016	2016–2017	2017–2018	2018–2019	2019–2020
Teacher of ELs	Employed	100	121	129	140	170
	Certified	219	272	304	353	391
	Difference	119	151	175	213	221
Bilingual teacher	Employed	44	28	25	32	24

Staff Type	Status	2015–2016	2016–2017	2017–2018	2018–2019	2019–2020
	Certified	85	66	61	58	56
	Difference	41	38	36	26	32
School psychologist	Employed	159	169	178	196	204
	Certified	163	178	185	203	209
	Difference	4	9	7	7	5
School social worker	Employed	21	19	23	25	38
	Certified	33	31	34	35	44
	Difference	12	12	11	10	6
Counselor	Employed	308	320	331	347	366
	Certified	683	727	749	769	797
	Difference	375	407	418	422	431
School reading specialist	Employed	116	109	99	107	106
	Certified	358	371	378	386	380
	Difference	242	262	279	279	274
Paraeducator	Employed	2,111	2,295	2,424	2,589	2,642
	Certified	2,396	2,661	2,796	3,019	3,092
	Difference	285	366	372	430	450
Special education teacher of students with disabilities (SWD)	Employed	1,746	1,863	1,923	2,030	2,169
	Certified	4,354	4,892	5,095	5,256	5,400
	Difference	2,608	3,029	3,172	3,226	3,231

SOURCE: Delaware Open Data, 2020a.

Given that the revealed focus of LEAs' Opportunity Fund and SSBG spending during 2019–2010 was on staff hires, several patterns in Figure 2.1 and Table 2.2 are particularly relevant to consider. The first is that there have been very few surplus certified bilingual teachers, school psychologists, and school social workers in the state; virtually all who hold that certificate in Delaware are actively employed in those roles. The second is that there have been very few bilingual teachers in the state (24) and few social workers (38) overall. Third, there is a surplus of staff certified as a teacher of ELs, counselors, reading interventionists, paraprofessionals,[7] and SPED teachers. With the exception of school psychologists and school social workers, in any

[7] In Delaware, *paraprofessionals*, or "paraeducators," are defined as public school employees who provide one-on-one small group instruction, assist with classroom management, provide assistance in computer labs and libraries/media centers, assist in training and support with functional skill activities, or provide instruction under the supervision of a teacher. Paraprofessionals are required to hold a high school diploma or General Educational Development (GED) certification, an associate degree or higher, and have a passing score on the ETS ParaPro assessment.

given year, there are roughly twice as many staff members possessing certifications for a given position than there are staff actively employed in a school at that position. For example, in 2019–2020, of the 380 individuals certified as school reading interventionists, only 106 were employed in Delaware schools.

Literature Review

In this section, we address the first research question by summarizing research that has assessed the effects on student outcomes of increases to school funding generally. We also summarize the efficacy of those categories of investments that the Opportunity Fund and SSBG support: increased spending to support LI, EL, and SPED students generally; reading interventionists; bilingual teachers; SPED for early grades; and mental health programming including social workers and SEL curriculum.

We conducted the literature review by first identifying meta-analyses and/or systematic reviews written since 2010 on each topical category we examine. When available, we use results from meta-analyses to describe the on-average effectiveness of these interventions. Lastly, drawing from the studies included in the each meta-analysis/systematic review in addition to our own search in electronic databases, such as the Education Research Information Center and Google Scholar, we highlight specific studies that either feature intervention impacts on student outcomes estimated using experimental or quasi-experimental methods or feature interventions with design aspects particularly relevant to the Delaware context.

Effectiveness of Increased Funding for Disadvantaged Students

Overall Relationships Between School Funding and Student Outcomes

The connection between school funding and student outcomes is a longstanding, fundamental topic for education researchers and policymakers. Although few, if any, would argue that money does not matter in an absolute sense for schools, there is a robust debate over the extent to which additional funds beyond a base amount influence outcomes and whether additional funds should be targeted to specific investments to improve student outcomes. As summarized in multiple reviews (Hanushek, 1981; Hanushek, 1986), early descriptive research on the topic produced in the 1960s, including the seminal Coleman Report (Coleman et al., 1966), suggested that differences in school resources did not explain much of the variation in student outcomes, after taking into account student demographic and socioeconomic factors. Although the accuracy of this conclusion is challenged by later studies applying different analytic techniques to the same set of studies (e.g., Hedges, Laine, and Greenwald, 1994), the notion that levels of school spending were unrelated to student outcomes became a popular view among education policymakers (Hanushek, 2003).

In recent years, several studies examining changes in school funding resulting from school finance reforms in the 1990s further challenged this interpretation (Candelaria and Shores, 2019; Jackson, Johnson, and Persico, 2016; LaFortune, Rothstein, and Schanzenbach, 2018). Importantly, this set of studies differs from prior research by using longitudinal data comparing outcomes of school districts prior to and after school finance reforms. For example, LaFortune, Rothstein, and Schanzenbach (2018), using a national longitudinal data set, found that, as a result of school finance reforms, districts saw an increase of $424 in per-pupil revenues and 0.10 standard deviation increase in student achievement ten years after the funding reform. Using a similar national data set, Jackson, Johnson, and Persico (2016) estimated that a 10 percent increase in per-pupil spending resulted, on average, in an increase of 0.3 completed years of education, 7 percent higher wages, and a 4 percentage point decrease in adult poverty. Jackson, Wigger, and Xiong (2018) explored how *decreases* in education spending resulting from the Great Recession of 2008 affected student outcomes, finding that a $1,000 decline in per-pupil spending resulted in a small (0.05 standard deviation) decrease in student test scores and a decrease in college-going by 3 percentage points.

Targeted School Funding for High-Need Students

Of course, the availability of more funding does not, in and of itself, lead to any change in student outcomes. Districts must carefully direct increases in funding toward those resources—perhaps via new staff, training existing staff, instructional materials, facilities, and other types of investments—that may in turn improve the learning conditions of students. What the prior evidence suggests is that, on average, districts have done well in directing funding toward investments that are meaningful for their enrolled students. However, this is not to suggest that all types of investments are equally effective in all settings nor that modest improvements in student outcomes always justify their costs. Understanding which types of schools, students, and investments to prioritize is highly influential in ultimately determining the efficacy of education spending. On the former, broadly, students in low-income districts appear to benefit the most from increases in school funding. Although the studies cited in the previous section found positive effects of school funding for the average district, both Candelaria and Shores (2019) and Jackson, Johnson, and Persico (2016) found that these effects are substantially larger within low-income schools and districts relative to the effects among students in higher-income schools and districts.

Driven by both equity and cost-effectiveness concerns, both federal and state governments have increased efforts to target education resources for disadvantaged students. At the federal level, funding for low-income students dates back to the inception of the Title I program, which grew out of the War on Poverty in 1965. The targeted funds are intended to support programs starting in preschool and continuing into the K–12 grades for schools with a high proportion of students in poverty. Subject to requirements designed to prevent supplantation, or displacement, of other state or local school funds by Title I monies, districts have considerable discretion regarding how funds are allocated across grades and between targeted programs within schools or school-wide programs. The most recent and rigorous evaluations of Title I funding suggest that the funds have had little to no overall significant effects on student outcomes (see Bitler and Karoly, 2015). Indeed, careful explorations of funding patterns suggest that Title I funds may be offset by other state and local funding, leaving little overall increases in per-pupil funding at Title I schools (Bitler and Karoly, 2015). An example of supplantation might include an LEA using Title I funds to pay for the salary of a reading interventionist during the 2019–2020 school year who was funded using state and/or local funds the year prior. Although a reading interventionist may be an appropriate support for low-income students, no new supports are afforded to low-income students because using Title I funds in this instance goes toward the maintenance of existing resources, rather than providing new resources. Such supplantation is difficult to avoid, despite accountability provisions designed to preclude it. Furthermore, districts may feel a need to demonstrate that Title I funds are being used on the margin for new purposes, which may push them toward more and more marginal interventions, rather than increasing funding for evidence-based approaches already being implemented.

In addition to federal Title I funds, states have also directed extra state funds to districts serving needy students through adopting weighted pupil funding programs, which provide additional per-pupil funding for students who fall under specific high-need categories, such as SPED, EL, and LI students (Foley, 2010), and through grant-based programs to which schools and districts serving higher proportions of high-need students can apply and receive supplemental funding. According to a 2012 report conducted by the Education Commission of the States (2012), virtually all states provide additional per-pupil funding for SPED students, and three-quarters of states provide additional funding for students who are classified as ELs or LI. Two examples of recent state funding programs for high-need students are particularly relevant to Delaware: the Disadvantaged Student Supplemental Fund in North Carolina (Henry, Fortner, and Thompson, 2010) and the Local Control Funding Formula in California (Johnson and Tanner, 2018). Both state programs provided additional funding for high-need students coupled with flexibility in how districts used the funds. Both resulted in improved student academic outcomes:

- In North Carolina, the Disadvantaged Student Supplemental Fund allocated an additional $22.4 million to 16 disadvantaged school districts, with eligibility for funds based on an index calculated using measures of teacher stability, teacher experience, student poverty rate, and proficiency rates. Eligible districts received an additional $250 per student and were required to direct funds toward a "menu" of 12 strategies listed by the state, but were given flexibility and local discretion to choose among them. The 12 broad strategies included class size reductions, performance and signing bonuses, and upgrading classroom materials and equipment. Comparing districts barely making and missing eligibility for the fund on the basis of their disadvantage index score, Henry, Fortner, and Thompson (2010) found that the additional $250 per pupil provided by the supplemental fund resulted in a modest increase of 0.1 standard deviation in test score performance among educationally disadvantaged students.

- In California, the "concentration grant" provision of the state's Local Control Funding Formula allocated additional funding to districts on the basis of the proportion of free or reduced-price lunch eligible, EL, and foster care students. Districts were required to submit loosely monitored "local control accountability plans" that outlined how these grants would improve services for high-need students. Johnson and Tanner (2018) found that, for each additional $1,000 increase in per-pupil spending experienced through this program, districts saw modest increases of 0.2 and 0.1 standard deviations in math and reading test scores, respectively, and a 6 percentage point increase in high school graduation rates.

Although the prior literature emphasizes both the average positive effects of increased school funding on student outcomes (Jackson, 2018) and the importance of allowing districts flexibility to allocate funds as they see fit (Jackson, 2018; Johnson and Tanner, 2018; Roza, Hagan, and Anderson, 2020), this is not to say that the effects of all types of spending have been shown to be equally effective. In their national analysis, Jackson, Johnson, and Persico (2016) found that the positive effects they identified of increased funding on student outcomes is, in large part, explained through corresponding reductions in class size, lower student-teacher ratios, and increases in instructional time. In particular, class size reductions enabled by additional funding have been linked in numerous studies to both students' short- and long-term positive outcomes, such as student test scores, educational attainment, and adult wages (Chetty et al., 2011; Gilraine, Macartney, and McMillan, 2020).[8]

By comparison, funding spent on capital investments have a more mixed record of impact, with no detected effects on student achievement in California (Cellini, Ferreira, and Rothstein, 2010; Martorell, Stange, and McFarlin, 2016) and Ohio (Goncalves, 2015) and positive effects in Ohio (Conlin and Thompson, 2017) and Michigan (Hong and Zimmer, 2016). Using longitudinal data on separate bond passages for operational and capital funding and educational outcomes in Wisconsin schools, Baron (2019) compared the effects of instructional and capital spending on student outcomes in the context of a single state. Districts narrowly passing operational bonds used primarily for increasing staff hires, staff salaries, and student support services saw medium-sized increases in standardized test scores (0.3 standard deviations) and a large reduction in high

[8] As noted in Jepsen and Rivkin (2009), the sudden increase in demand for staff linked to class-size mandates can result in a shortage of qualified, experienced staff, dampening the positive effect of class-size reductions—a factor that should be taken into consideration when implementing programs to hire new staff.

school dropout rates (25 percent reduction). By contrast, bonds passed specifically for increased capital outlays saw no corresponding change in these same outcomes, reinforcing the pattern found through separate studies that direct spending that is specifically toward students and staff is most effective for improving student outcomes.

An often-asked question regards the relative effectiveness of certain types of instructional spending, such as the benefits of hiring new staff compared with providing additional professional development (PD) for existing staff or comparing the merits of purchasing new curriculum or new supplies for improving student outcomes. This is an important question but one for which education research lacks an answer. This is because the question is difficult to address both empirically and substantively. First, although many of the studies just referenced use credible designs to estimate the effects of districts receiving additional funds, they typically do not allow for a rigorous estimate of the effect of specific uses of funds beyond broad instructional-versus-capital classifications, such as what is used in Baron (2019). As is the case with the Opportunity Fund, most funding programs encourage LEAs, within broad guidelines, to use funds as they see best fit. And most LEAs enact many types of investments at once, not in isolation, making it difficult to parse the contribution of each individual type of investment. A second, related point is that the effectiveness of any single investment will work in concert with other new investments in addition to existing school resources. For example, the effective adoption of curriculum will be dependent on high-quality teaching staff, access to material-specific PD, and the presence of aligned assessments (Polikoff et al., 2020). The intertwined nature of school resources further emphasizes the importance of local flexibility in directing funds toward areas of need.

Effectiveness of Specific Interventions for High-Need Students

The previous section of our literature review summarized prior empirical evidence that shows, on average, that increases to school funding result in improvements to student outcomes, spending on instruction is typically more aligned to improvements than capital spending, and these improvements are greater for districts serving larger proportions of high-need and LI students. In this section, we examine the research about types of investments made within the areas targeted by the Opportunity Fund and SSBG: (1) reading interventionists, (2) student mental health and SEL supports, (3) SPED, and (4) supports for ELs. We also provide examples of interventions in each category that have been proven to be effective.

Effectiveness of Reading Interventionists

Reading interventionists have varied responsibilities depending on the school, district, and state in which they work (Quatroche, Bena, and Hamilton, 2001). Generally, reading interventionists support and extend traditional classroom instruction by providing (1) direct instruction to students through pull-out classes or serving as teachers of record or (2) PD or coaching on reading instruction to other staff.

The meta-analyses of direct reading interventions writ large (not just reading interventionists) suggest that supports directed toward struggling readers result in moderately sized positive effects on their reading skills. Reviews of prior literature in grades K–3 (Wanzek et al., 2018) and grades 4–12 (Scammacca et al., 2015; Wanzek et al., 2013) found that students needing and receiving reading interventions saw modest- to medium-sized improvements of 0.1–0.3 standard deviations on reading assessments relative to similar students not receiving those interventions. Interventions focused on developing student vocabulary, compared with interventions focused on comprehension, fluency, or word study, yielded the largest overall effects on reading achievement. The effects of reading interventions were typically largest among elementary and middle school classrooms (Scammacca et al., 2015). Counterintuitively, interventions that provided 26 hours or more of reading services were less effective than ones providing fewer hours, which the researchers hypothesized could be because students who had briefer interventions had to more frequently extrapolate their strategies to less-familiar texts. Wanzek et al. (2018) did not find significant differences in effectiveness in whether general education teachers, reading interventionists, or paraprofessionals administered the specific interventions across the studies they reviewed, suggesting that the specific certification of the interventionist did not have an effect.

Regarding reading interventionists serving as teacher coaches, Kraft, Blazar, and Hogan's review (2018) indicated that, across 60 studies of teacher coaching programs, access to coaching for teachers was significantly associated with both positive changes to measures of classroom instruction (average, large-effect size of 0.5 standard deviations) and reading achievement (average, medium-effect size of 0.2 standard deviations). The authors found that teacher coaching was most effective when paired with group trainings to build foundational instructional skills or paired with specific curricula or instructional materials, implying that coaching is more effective when situated with other components of a coherent instructional system. The authors did not find any relationship between the total hours of coaching received and effects on either teacher instruction or student outcomes.

Effectiveness of Mental Health and Social and Emotional Learning Interventions

Investments to support students' mental health and social-emotional development were common among LEAs' Opportunity Fund investments. Although several studies identify high schoolers' access to counseling as an important factor in promoting high school graduation and postsecondary attendance (Castleman and Goodman, 2018; Hurwitz and Howell, 2013; Mulhern, 2020), less work has been done about the impacts that counselors and social workers have on elementary-age students, which are the focus of our study.

We identified three studies of elementary school counselors. Reback (2010a) used data from two nationally representative surveys, the Early Childhood Longitudinal Survey-Kindergarten Cohort and the Schools and Staffing Survey, and found that changes to state policies regarding mandatory counselor-to-student ratios yielded increases in the percentage of K–3 students receiving counseling and modest improvements of roughly 0.1 standard deviations in math and reading test scores and measures of social and emotional skills (e.g., externalizing problem behaviors, internalizing problem behaviors) of these students. In a separate study, Reback (2010b), using Alabama state data, found that increased counselor funding resulted in less-frequent disciplinary incidents but had no effects on student achievement. Lastly, Carrell and Hoekstra (2014) examined the relationship between counselors and student outcomes in schools in a Florida county. Using within-school variation in counseling staff over time, the authors found modest effects: having an additional counselor increased boys' math and reading achievement by more than 1 percentile point and decreased the number of disciplinary infractions for both boys (0.015 fewer infractions) and girls (0.09 fewer infractions).

These consistent effects of counselors on behavioral and disciplinary outcomes are particularly important given the evidence of negative spillover effects on students in classrooms with higher proportions of classmates diagnosed with emotional and behavioral disorders (Fletcher, 2010; Gottfried, Egalite, and Kirksey, 2016; Gottfried and Harven, 2015). Thus, providing social, emotional, and behavioral supports for students through counselors and other school-based staff yields both direct and indirect benefits for students in the schools they serve.

Another promising example that involved the use of school-based student nonacademic support services was the City Connects program implemented in Boston Public Schools. This intervention entailed schools employing school site coordinators, who were formally trained and licensed as school counselors or social workers, to coordinate services through collaboration with schools, families, and community agencies. The evaluation of this program found that, relative to demographically similar students in elementary and middle schools that did not participate in the program, elementary and middle school students in program schools saw higher class grades in both ELA and math (moderate to large effect sizes ranging from 0.19 to 0.34 depending on grade and subject) and on the middle school state assessment (moderate to large effect sizes ranging from 0.15 to 0.45) (Walsh et al., 2014). In a follow-up study, Lee–St. John et al. (2018) found that students participating in City Connects during elementary and middle school were 7 percentage points less likely to drop out of high school compared with non-participants; in their benefit-cost analysis of the program, Bowden et al. (2015) estimated that the program resulted in a total of $3 in benefits for every $1 in cost, suggesting that counselor and social worker investments can yield substantial benefits.

Beyond dedicated staff, another avenue through which schools can support holistic student development is through the use of curricula and programming that specifically aim to develop students' SEL skills. SEL covers a broad range of competencies and skills that focus on noncognitive development, trauma-informed learning, character development, and social skills. SEL activities can include curriculum development, out-of-school time programming, family engagement, and PD for teachers in both teaching and using SEL skills.

The 2018 American Educator Panel, a nationally representative survey of teachers, indicated that the majority of teachers have already adopted some type of SEL initiative, practice, or program in their schools and have received in-service training on SEL (Hamilton, Doss, and Steiner, 2019). Furthermore, reviews of research literature broadly found that exposure to SEL activities typically led to increases in not only SEL skills but also achievement outcomes. For example, Durlak et al. (2011) reviewed a total of 213 SEL interventions and found that participation in these interventions was associated, on average, with moderate to large effect sizes of 0.6 for student SEL skills, 0.3 for student academic, and 0.2 for students' conduct problems, attitudes, and positive social behaviors. Additionally, researchers have found that the effects of participating in SEL interventions is durable. Taylor et al. (2017) conducted a review of the effects of SEL interventions measured at least six months after student participation and found slightly smaller but still significant effects on the same categories of outcomes identified by Durlak et al. (2011). One common moderating factor identified by both reviews is student age, with the effect of SEL programs typically being smaller for older students, suggesting that these programs are maximally effective for students in elementary school.

Effectiveness of English Learner Interventions

A major emphasis of the Opportunity Fund program is to provide additional supports for students who are ELs, with LEAs proposing a mixture of hiring additional staff to support EL students, offering EL-focused PD for existing staff, and adapting instructional materials specifically for EL students. Broadly, the literature suggests that direct intervention programs for EL students and EL PD for teachers coupled with a specific curriculum or intervention are the most impactful investments for EL students.

Several studies indicate that students benefit from participating in small group reading intervention programs, with the impacts of these programs being generally larger for EL students than non-EL students (Hanover Research, 2015; Lesaux et al., 2014; Ludwig, Guo, and Georgiou, 2019). A meta-analysis of the effects of reading interventions specifically for EL students conducted by Ludwig, Guo, and Georgiou (2019) found large effects on reading accuracy (average effect size = 1.2 standard deviations), reading fluency (0.8 standard deviations), and reading comprehension (0.5 standard deviations) for EL students participating in multisession interventions that occurred in addition to regular classroom instruction.

Additionally, there is evidence that PD for teachers geared toward specific EL interventions can be beneficial. For example, using a pre-post design, Matuchniak, Olson, and Scarcella (2014) saw significantly higher gains to EL student writing (large effect size of 0.44 of a standard deviation) for students assigned to teachers participating in the Pathway Project PD program on

EL students' writing skills. Similarly, August et al. (2009) evaluated Quality English and Science Teaching, a curriculum and PD program designed to improve science knowledge among EL, and found modest-sized effects of 0.15 of a standard deviation among EL students.

One challenge of supporting EL students is recruiting and hiring staff with the skills and qualifications necessary to teach these students. Master et al. (2016) found evidence that teachers are differentially effective teaching EL and non-EL students, which suggests that schools and LEAs must consider teacher effectiveness specifically with regard to the EL population when making staffing decisions. Furthermore, Master et al. (2016) found teachers' access to pre-service and in-service EL-focused PD is related to teachers' differential effectiveness for EL students, providing that additional support that EL PD may be a worthwhile investment for LEAs. Lastly, several studies indicate that bilingual education improves or is at least neutral to students' English proficiency, suggesting that teachers who are fluent in the home languages of their students are valuable for supporting EL students (August and Shanahan, 2006; Slavin et al., 2011).

Effectiveness of Special Education Interventions

Special education interventions take several forms: primary prevention, secondary prevention, individualized interventions, and tertiary prevention. Primary prevention is delivered in general education settings; secondary prevention consists of small-group intervention, such as tutoring, progress monitoring, and structured teaching; and tertiary prevention is primarily individualized interventions, such as specific learning disability identification and Individualized Education Program–based intervention (Benner et al., 2010; Reschly, 2005).

The majority of research on SPED focuses on the more intensive secondary and tertiary tiers of intervention, with the exception of Positive Behavior and Intervention Supports (PBIS), which can be used either as a primary or secondary intervention. PBIS provides teachers with additional training and other resources to address a range of student behavioral needs (Benner et al., 2010; Ihlo and Nantais, 2010). PBIS trainings typically involve helping teachers develop and define behavioral expectations, teach the expectations, provide positive reinforcement, and supply consequences and supports for behavioral issues (Ihlo and Nantais, 2010). PBIS interventions delivered in single-classroom settings led to statistically significant reductions in students' thought problems, attention problems, and aggression (Benner et al., 2010). Other studies found that schools using PBIS saw a decrease in student behavior issues, suspensions, and expulsions (Barrett, Bradshaw, and Lewis-Palmer, 2008; Bradshaw, Mitchell, and Leaf, 2010; Horner et al., 2009). For example, Barrett, Bradshaw, and Lewis-Palmer (2008) found that, after the adoption of a PBIS PD program in Maryland, suspension rates in both elementary and middle schools declined by 2 and 7 percentage points, respectively.

Tertiary interventions typically involve individualized interaction with students and thus are focused on helping instructors develop specific instructional methods for SPED students. In a meta-analysis, Swanson and Hoskyn (1998) classify interventions as therapeutic, remedial, direct instruction, or cognitive strategy instruction, finding that that direct ($d = 0.91$) and strategy instruction ($d = 1.07$) produced large effects in student reading, achievement, and social emotional outcomes and were more effective than remedial and therapeutic interventions.

In most SPED teacher training programs, teachers are taught strategies and methods for teaching SPED students but lack training in co-teaching and creating lesson plans for general education teachers and content areas (Bryant et al., 2001; Jenkins and Yoshimura, 2010; Leko and Brownell, 2009). Given the fact that SPED teachers often work with general education teachers or push into general education settings, high-quality on-the-job training and PD about co-teaching and co-planning are important for these teachers. In their 2017 meta-analysis of effective PD for SPED teachers, Brock and Carter (2017) found that PD that included either performance feedback or that modeled different strategies tended to be more effective, and PD that included both elements were most effective. The authors did not find a relationship between efficacy and duration of PD.

Summary of Literature

The existing evidence indicates that, on average, increases to school funding were linked to improvements to student outcomes, with larger effects among the LEAs with the highest shares of students who qualify for a free or reduced price meal. Additionally, some studies suggest that changes to funding programs that increase LEA's discretion in how to use funds are also associated with improvements to student outcomes. This evidence supports the notion that the increased funding offered by the flexible Opportunity Fund in particular has reason to result in at least some positive effect on student outcomes.

That said, the evidence does not suggest that all types of district expenditures are equally effective. The evidence points to instructional investments, such as increases in the number of staff, staff compensation, reduced class sizes, and increases to instructional time, being more robustly related to student learning than school capital investments. Indeed, when examining the research on specific interventions proven most effective for supporting the different types of students (e.g., ELs, students with disabilities) or student needs (e.g., reading supports, mental health) targeted by the Opportunity Fund and SSBG programs, the most impactful interventions often required a combination of both trained staff and high-quality instructional materials. As we describe in Chapter 3, the focus across all four Delaware funding streams—flexible Opportunity Fund, mental health Opportunity Funds, SSBG reading interventionists, and SSBG K–3 SPED—on staff and PD investments have promise.

In this first of three annual reports, the first portion of the funding-outcomes relationship explored the extent to which Delaware LEAs use their available Opportunity Fund and SSBG funding and toward what types of investments did LEAs direct these funds. Reports in subsequent years will examine whether this influx of funding was associated with differences in student outcomes and to what extent differences in how LEAs used these funds are predictive of the changes, if any, in their students' outcomes.

3. Data and Methods

We draw on information from multiple LEA-level data sources to describe LEAs' proposed investments using funds provided by the Opportunity Fund and SSBG, the implementation status of these investments, and LEA leaders' self-perceived best practices regarding the use of the Opportunity Fund and SSBG funds. We use a combination of LEA applications for funds, two brief surveys of LEA leaders in 2019–2020, and administrative from DDOE about LEA expenditures, SSBG reading interventionists, and student enrollment and staff characteristics. These data sources are described in further detail in this chapter.

In combination, these data offer a wide-reaching but still limited view of Opportunity Fund and SSBG program implementation. Because the two surveys of LEA leaders were brief (about five minutes each) and because we have not yet collected qualitative data via LEA interviews and case studies, we lack some depth of information about the reasons for some of the patterns we see in LEA use (or not) of funds, barriers to investments, and COVID-19 adaptations. However, the existing data we collect in our research for this report provide a broad picture of LEAs' use of the Opportunity Fund and SSBG programs during the 2019–2020 school year.

School Year 2019–2020 Opportunity Fund Applications

LEAs interested in using flexible Opportunity Funds in the 2019–2020 school year were required to submit an application detailing which investments the funds would be used for, approximate costs for each investment, and metrics that would be used to evaluate the efficacy of each investment. These applications were due to the DDOE by June 2019.

Similarly, LEAs wishing to obtain Opportunity Funds for mental health supports for qualifying schools were also required to submit an application to the DDOE by August 2019. LEAs submitted a separate application for each school, and, of the 45 total applications, 44 were approved (the remaining application was merged with another school's application).

We coded both the flexible fund and mental health support applications to identify the types of investments that LEAs proposed and the proposed cost of each investment. In addition, we recorded the metrics that applicants proposed to use to track the investments for the flexible Opportunity Fund applications. More specifically, we categorized potential Opportunity Fund investments into one of six categories: (1) hiring of additional **staff**, (2) purchasing **PD** or training for existing staff, (3) purchasing **curricula** or other types of instructional materials, (4) offering out-of-school (e.g., afterschool, summer school) **programming** for students and their families, (5) providing classroom **supplies**, and (6) **other** miscellaneous investments.

Because the majority of investments propose the hiring of new staff, we also created subcategories of staff investments that identify the specific role or purpose of each new staff member. These staff subcategories include (1) staff for supporting **EL and bilingual students**, including English as a second language (ESL)–certified teachers, translators, and biliteracy coaches; (2) staff for supporting **students' socioemotional and behavioral skills**, such as social workers, school counselors, and student-family liaisons; (3) staff for providing **academic support**, such as reading and math interventionists and instructional coaches; (4) **paraprofessionals**; and (5) **general** unspecified staff and **other** miscellaneous staff. To create mutually exclusive categories, we coded any staff investment as *EL/bilingual support staff* if it was designated to specifically serve EL students even if the investment can be potentially coded into other categories (e.g., EL paraprofessional, bilingual social worker). We use these same categories to classify LEA leaders' answers about investments in the April 2020 RAND survey, LEA leaders' replies at the end of the 2019–2020 school year on the final summative survey, and the conference conducted by the Office of the Secretary of Education.

School Year 2019–2020 SSBG Reading Interventionists Staffing File and Survey

The DDOE collected the names and email addresses of the 45 reading interventionists that qualifying elementary schools hired. The DDOE shared this file and results from a winter 2020 survey that the DDOE fielded to the reading interventionists with us. Thirty-three reading interventionists responded to the survey (73 percent response rate). The online survey included 17 questions and focused on the interventionists' qualifications, years of experience, comfort level with teaching elementary-age reading concepts, and professional learning preferences. We draw on these survey results to summarize the interventionists' experience levels.

April 2020 RAND Survey

RAND fielded an online survey to each of the 40 participating LEAs in April 2020 for one month, closing the survey on May 1, 2020. Each LEA was responsible for completing one survey. To reduce the burden placed on LEA respondents, we prepopulated the surveys with either the investments that the LEA had listed in its flexible Opportunity Fund application or, if available, an updated list of investments derived from the midyear conference that the DDOE held with each LEA leader.[9] We used this list of proposed investments to ask the LEA leader

---

[9] In January 2020, traditional district superintendents met individually in person with the Office of the Secretary of Education, and charter LEA superintendents met with the Charter School Office at the DDOE. Prior to and during

respondent six questions about each investment, including the status of each, barriers (if any) to completing the investment, whether the investment served a single or multiple schools, and the perceived effectiveness of the investments.

The survey contained six questions about individual investments that the LEAs had made using the Opportunity Fund and another five questions about the SSBG reading interventionists or SPED formula funding. The survey took approximately ten minutes to complete, and we did not offer a financial incentive. We received a total of 37 responses (90 percent response rate), with the three nonrespondents being charter LEAs. Additionally, not all LEA respondents provided responses for each of their Opportunity Fund investments. Of 185 total Opportunity Fund investments proposed, respondents provided responses to 86 percent of them; we did not find evidence that the rates of missingness significantly differed between traditional and charter LEAs or the student composition (e.g., race/ethnicity, free or reduced-price lunch) of the LEA.

Prework Survey and Notes from the DDOE Summative Conferences with LEAs

We captured LEA leaders' end-of-year school year 2019–2020 perceptions of their Opportunity Fund and SSBG investments from an online survey we developed for LEA leaders to pre-fill in preparation for the final conference they held with the Office of the Secretary of Education. We coordinated with the Office of the Secretary of Education to develop an online survey protocol that covered the implementation status of the Opportunity Fund and SSBG investments. Specifically, the conference (and thus the preparatory survey) centered on LEA leaders' end-of-year perceptions of best practices for improving academic achievement specifically for EL students, LI students, SPED students, and any best practices specifically concerning the hiring of mental health and reading interventionists using Opportunity Fund or SSBG funds. Because of the COVID-19 pandemic, the DDOE also asked the LEA leaders how they altered their Opportunity Fund and SSBG investments in light of the transition to the remote learning in Delaware.

The Office of the Secretary of Education sent out the online survey, requesting that LEA leaders fill it advance of the summative conference. The Office of the Secretary of Education then used the answers from the survey to structure the summative conference conversation. At the Office of the Secretary of Education conference, the Secretary of Education also filled out missing information, if any, in hard copy. Upon completion, the Office of the Secretary of Education provided us with typed notes of each conference. We used these notes to verify

---

the meeting, the superintendents went through each of the Opportunity Fund application investments they proposed, discussing the status of each, which schools received the investments, challenges with the investments, and most effective investments and plans to modify them. We coded this information and used it in the April 2020 survey.

information captured in LEA leaders' responses in the preparatory survey for the summative conference and to fill in missing information. After filling in missing data, 36 of 40 LEAs had complete survey data about the final status of the Opportunity Fund and SSBG investments.

Expenditure Data

To assess spending, we draw on expenditure data from the final validity report provided by the DDOE for fiscal year (FY) 2020. The validity report contains all federal, state, and local expenditures at the district level by fund type and appropriation code.[10]

Because school expenditure data are not uniformly collected at the school level, we instead analyze spending at only the district level for all four programs, even for the SSBG K–3 SPED program and the Opportunity Grant mental health funds, which are allocated at the school level.[11] Because we are examining the first year of implementation only, we do not analyze year-on-year trends in expenditures. We intend to, however, do so in future reports to assess whether the rate of carrying over funds into the next year escalates and whether the additional funding from the two program streams supplants rather than adds to overall district expenditures.

Delaware School-Level Student and Staff Characteristics Data

We use LEA- and school-level student enrollment data from the 2017–2018, 2018–2019, and 2019–2020 school years to describe the student populations (e.g., LI, EL, SWD, Black and Latino students) at each LEA and calculate per-pupil expenditures across the Opportunity Fund and SSBG funding streams. Additionally, to describe Delaware staffing patterns, we use state-level data on the total number of FTEs who are certified and/or employed in Delaware public schools from 2015–2016 to 2019–2020. We obtained student characteristic and staff employment data from the Delaware Open Data Portal and state-level staff certification data from the DDOE.

---

[10] For Opportunity Fund expenditures, we examine appropriation codes 05297, 08914 (flexible funding), and 08915 and 05311 (mental health funding). For SSBG K–3 basic SPED expenditures, we examine appropriation code 05309, and for SSBG reading interventionists, we examine appropriation code 05310.

[11] Because we examine only the most recent school year expenditures (2019–2020), we have not converted the spending to real dollars. However, we do intend to do so when examining expenditures over two and three years in our future reports.

4. Findings

Local Educational Agency Expenditures on the Opportunity Fund and SSBG Programs

In this chapter, we address the second research question: How much did LEAs expend on the Opportunity Fund and SSBG? In 2019–2020, the legislature appropriated to each funding stream the amounts shown in Table 4.1, totaling $33.5 million. Of this total, LEAs and the DDOE expended $25.9 million, leaving about 23 percent unspent and eligible for expenditure in future years. The mental health program had the greatest proportion of unspent funding, while the SSBG reading interventionists had the least. In Table A.2, we list FY 2020 expenditures of each of the 40 LEAs that received Opportunity Funds, the SSBG, or both.

Table 4.1. Opportunity Fund and SSBG Expenditures in Fiscal Year 2020

Program	Total State Appropriation for FY 2020	Total Expenditures by Local Educational Agencies*	Percentage Unspent, Available for Future Spending
The Opportunity Fund, flexible	$20,000,000	$14,953,803	24%**
The Opportunity Fund, mental health	$5,000,000	$3,476,626	30%
SSBG K–3 SPED	$4,489,700	$3,364,190	25%
SSBG reading interventionists	$3,974,000	$3,860,601	3%

SOURCE: DDOE validity report provided to the authors, current as of June 30, 2020.
NOTES: *Total expenditures in FY 2020 include funds that had been appropriated in prior fiscal years but spent in 2020. **Although there were only LEA expenditures for the other three programs, Opportunity Fund flexible funding included $250,000 of non-LEA expenditures, which is accounted for in this percentage of unspent funds.

The overall spending patterns in Table 4.1 and the LEA-level expenditures in Table A.2 mask the substantial range in expenditures when expressed on a per-pupil or per-school basis. In Figures 4.1–4.4, we plot the distribution of LEAs' expenditures divided by the number of targeted students or schools by each funding stream—i.e., by the number of EL and/or LI students for the flexible Opportunity Funds; K–3 SPED students for the SSBG SPED funding; and qualifying, disadvantaged schools in the LEA for the Opportunity Fund mental health and reading interventionist program. Next, we describe the results shown in Figures 4.1 and 4.2, which show the two programs that allocate funds on a per-pupil basis.

For the **flexible Opportunity Funds**, the 40 LEAs' expenditures ranged from a low of $141 per disadvantaged student to as high as $514 per disadvantaged student. The average per-pupil spending was $249. This average is lower than the intended expenditure of $500 per EL and $300 per LI student. We arrived at these figures by dividing each LEA's flexible Opportunity

Fund expenditures by the sum of LI and EL students in 2019–2020.[12] Only two out of ten LEAs had per-pupil expenditures between the intended $300–$500 range, and two out of three LEAs had per-pupil expenditures below $300 per LI and EL student. Charter LEAs (which had one school) tended to have higher per-pupil flexible Opportunity Fund expenditures than traditional public school districts, which also meant that charter LEAs were less likely to have large amounts of unspent funds.

We hypothesize two reasons why the expenditures per LI and EL students fell below the intended levels for most LEAs. The first is that only one-third of LEAs fully expended their available flexible Opportunity Funds. Of those LEAs, they expended an average of $297 per pupil. Among the two-thirds of LEAs that had unspent funds, they spent an average of $245 per pupil and had $216,859 in unspent funds. The largest unspent funding amount for any single LEA was $1,438,888 in the Christina School District at the end of 2019–2020. The second is that the expended flexible Opportunity Funds monies typically fell below the intended levels because of the increase in the number of EL and LI students from 2018–2019 (which was the DDOE's basis for funding allocations to LEAs) to 2019–2020. A net increase in the sum of EL and LI students spreads the allocation of flexible Opportunity Funds over more students and thus lowers the per-pupil allocation.

[12] Because the DDOE does not allocate funding for EL students separately from LI students, we are not able to examine per-pupil expenditures for each student subgroup. Although the DDOE allocated funding based on prior-year, and not current year, student enrollments, we examine 2019–2020 expenditures divided by 2019–2020 enrollments to understand the spending variation across LEAs in terms of actual number of students served.

Figure 4.1. LEA Expenditures per Disadvantaged Pupil* of Flexible Opportunity Funds in Fiscal Year 2020

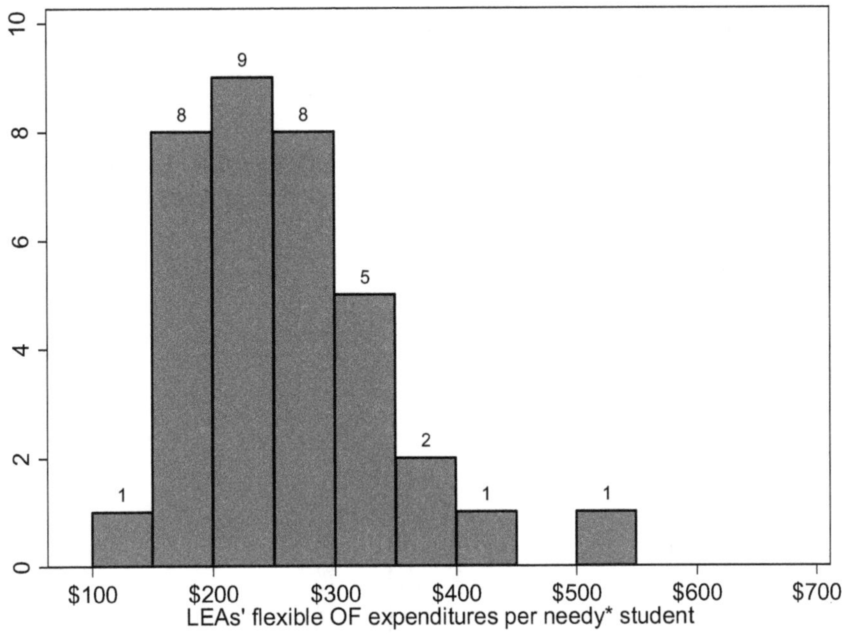

SOURCES: FY 2020 validity file provided to the authors; Delaware Open Data, 2020b.
NOTES: Forty LEAs received Opportunity Fund flexible monies in 2019–2020. *Expenditures are shown as total flexible Opportunity Fund expenditures divided by the sum of LI and EL students in the LEA as of 2019–2020. OF = Opportunity Fund.

As shown in Figure 4.2, **SSBG expenditures for K–3 SPED students** varied across LEAs more than flexible Opportunity Funds. For flexible Opportunity Funds, the ratio of highest to lowest spending by LEAs ($514 and $141 per pupil, respectively) was about 3.7. In contrast, for SSBG SPED funds, that ratio was about seven, with the highest and lowest spending by LEAs per K–3 SPED student at $1,118 and $147, respectively. Although both the flexible Opportunity Funds and SSBG SPED funding were allocated proportionally by the number of qualified pupils, the wide variation observed in per-pupil SSBG expenditures can be explained by the fact that many LEAs did not spend some of the funds they received, and there was substantial variation in the number of eligible students across years. Proportionally, single-school charter LEAs can have greater fluctuation year-on-year in eligible students than traditional school districts given their small number of enrolled K–3 SPED students. As with the flexible Opportunity Fund dollars, charter LEAs (which had one school per LEA) had higher per-pupil expenditures than traditional public schools, with a few exceptions. They were also the LEAs with the least amount of unexpended funds.

Ten of the 27 LEAs that received these funds expended them fully.[13] Traditional public school districts, which had larger numbers of schools than charter LEAs, were the least likely to expend the funds fully. The 17 LEAs that did not spend all of their funds left $103,293 unspent on average. The most unspent dollars were again in the Christina School District, with $472,954 unspent.

Figure 4.2. LEA Expenditures per K–3 Special Education Student of SSBG Special Education Funds in Fiscal Year 2020

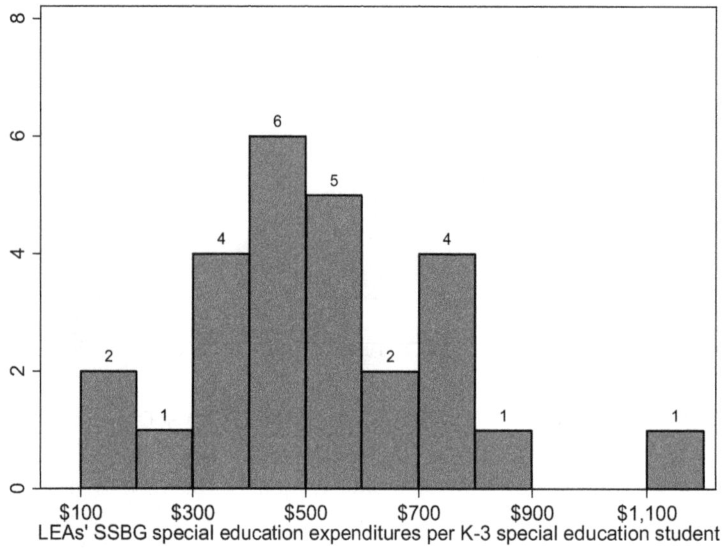

SOURCES: FY 2020 validity file provided to the authors; Delaware Open Data, 2020b.

NOTES: Twenty-seven LEAs expended SSBG SPED funding in 2019–2020. Expenditures shown as total LEA expenditure of SSBG K–3 SPED funds divided by the number of K–3 SPED enrollees in 2019–2020. We exclude two LEAs where counts of SPED students per grade were less than five and thus redacted.

Figure 4.3 examines the distribution of **mental health Opportunity Fund** expenditures per school in 2019–2020 across the 15 LEAs that received these funds. The expenditures ranged from $23,553 to $159,777, with the average spending at $91,320. Like the SSBG reading specialist program, this program did not allocate funds on a per-pupil basis. Instead, the DDOE reviewed and approved applications that LEAs submitted for their qualifying schools. But this particular program had greater inequity in per-school funding than the SSBG reading specialist program because that program prespecified one FTE staff per qualifying school, whereas this one

[13] An additional two LEAs (Caesar Rodney School District and Woodbrige School District) expended $0 of these funds in FY 2020 but had prior-year allocations that had rolled into FY 2020 and again rolled over to FY 2021.

did not. This wide range in mental health Opportunity Fund per-school expenditures mainly reflects two factors: (1) the substantial variation in the services that LEAs proposed and funding they requested in their applications to the DDOE, which is then amplified by (2) the variation in salary levels of staff hired using these funds (which reflects their years of experience and training and LEA salary schedules). For example, Academia Antonia Alonso Charter School proposed hiring two full-time SEL specialists and one full-time paraprofessional and recruiting AmeriCorps members to implement a reading intervention program in the single charter school. Meanwhile, the Colonial School District proposed to hire one full-time reading interventionist for Pleasantville Elementary School. Even if two applications had requested the same investment (e.g., one new FTE hire), corresponding expenditures may still differ if those two hires differ substantially in terms of experience and qualifications and if LEAs' pay scales differ substantially. In the 44 applications for mental health funding, the number of requested investments ranged from one to six, and the requested amount ranged from $46,956 to $257,784. Charter LEAs typically spent more mental health Opportunity Funds per school than did traditional public school districts. However, there was no strong pattern in the type of LEA that had the greatest amount of unspent funds, perhaps because the method of allocation for this funding was driven by LEA requests rather than per-pupil allocations.

Figure 4.3. LEA Expenditures per Qualifying School* of Mental Health Opportunity Fund in Fiscal Year 2020

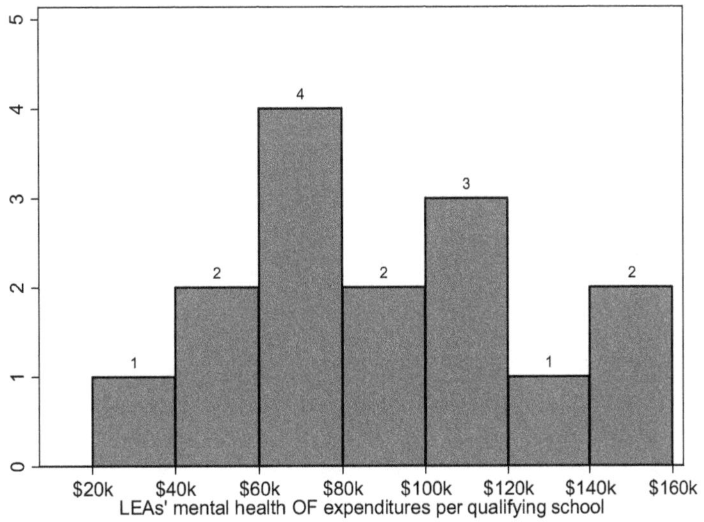

SOURCES: FY 2020 validity file and Opportunity Fund mental health applications provided to the authors.
NOTES: Fifteen LEAs received Opportunity Fund mental health supports in 2019–2020. *The spending shown is the total per-LEA expenditures of mental health Opportunity Funds divided by the number of qualifying elementary schools that applied and were approved. OF = Opportunity Fund.

Figure 4.4 shows the distribution of LEA expenditures on **SSBG reading interventionists** per school across the 15 LEAs that received these funds. The expenditures range from $41,331 to $119,165. As described in Chapter 2, unlike the Opportunity Fund mental health supports for which LEAs must apply, the DDOE distributed SSBG funds to LEAs that housed the 45 qualifying schools in 2019–2020. The funds covered up to one FTE reading interventionist position per school. The variation in Figure 4.4 reflects the variation in the salaries of the reading interventionists (which is based on their experience, qualification levels, and LEA salary schedule) and the actual FTE (e.g., half-time versus full-time) allocated to the interventionists.

According to the winter 2020 survey that the DDOE administered to the interventionists, the 33 respondents reported varying but generally high levels of experience and training. Their teaching experience ranged from as few as two to more than 20 years, with about three-quarters having more than ten years and only two less than five years of experience. About half of the respondents had either a master's or doctoral degree in reading and literacy or were pursuing a master's degree in this field.

Unlike the other three programs, we do not observe a pattern of charter LEAs spending the most per school or having the least unexpended funds. Recall that this is a program in which LEAs in aggregate spent down 97 percent of the overall allocation to support the hire of one FTE reading interventionist per school. Three of the 15 LEAs fully expended their funding (one of these was Christina School District, which had the greatest amount of unexpended flexible Opportunity Funds and SSBG SPED funds). The average LEA left $23,724 unspent, and Red Clay School District had the largest amount of unspent funds—$180,361.

Figure 4.4. LEA Expenditures per Opportunity Fund Qualifying School* of SSBG Reading Interventionist Funds in Fiscal Year 2020

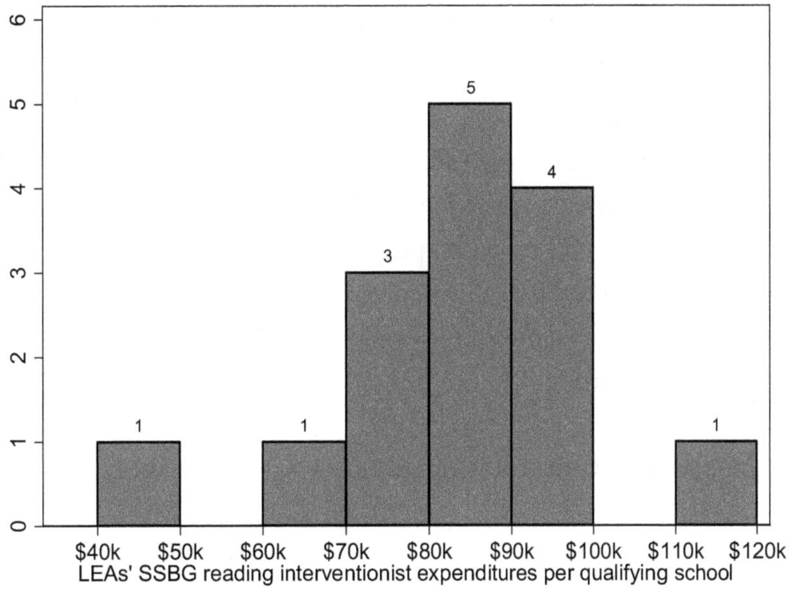

SOURCE: FY 2020 validity file and DDOE 2020 SSBG reading interventionists roster provided to the authors.
NOTES: Fifteen LEAs received SSBG reading interventionist funding in 2019–2020. *The spending shown is the total per-LEA expenditures of SSBG reading interventionist funds divided by the number of schools per LEA in DDOE records with a reading interventionist.

Local Educational Agency Investments Using Opportunity Funds and SSBG Funds

In this section, we discuss the portion of the second research question pertaining to the different investments that leaders indicated their LEA planned and made with the Opportunity Fund and SSBG monies.

Opportunity Fund—Flexible Funding Investments

In our review of flexible Opportunity Fund applications for 2019–2020, 40 Delaware LEAs received DDOE approval for 185 separate investments (an average of 4.6 investments per LEA), such as hiring an SEL specialist and purchasing a curriculum. The number of proposed investments ranged from one investment (11 LEAs) to 17 investments. Three traditional school districts requested over ten investments: Appoquinimink School District (17 investments), Christina School District (15), and Colonial School District (15). Investments by these three districts accounted for one-quarter of the 185 total investments.

We categorized each investment into one of six categories, as described in Chapter 3. Table 4.2 shows that the most frequently requested investment type by far was hiring new staff, such as teachers, interventionists, and counselors (54 percent of all proposed investments). The second most frequent request was for additional PD and training for existing staff (15 percent). The most popular topics for PD were ESL instruction, trauma-informed practices, and training in a specific curriculum or instructional material (e.g., Achieve 3000, Benchmark ELA, Springboard). Other common planned uses for flexible Opportunity Funds were purchasing curriculum and other instructional and intervention materials (11 percent), such as the assessment aimsweb and ESL-specific instructional materials; followed by providing additional in-school and out-of-school programming for students and families (10 percent), such as summer camps and family engagement activities; and purchasing school and classroom supplies (7 percent), such as smartboards, laptops, and furniture.

Table 4.2. Categories of Approved Opportunity Fund Investments, 2019–2020 (*n* = 185)

Category	Percentage	*n*
Staff	54	100
PD	15	27
Curriculum	11	20
Programming	10	19
Supplies	7	13
Other	3	6

SOURCE: LEA flexible Opportunity Fund applications provided to the authors.
NOTES: Forty LEAs were approved to make 185 different investments.

Among the 100 flexible Opportunity Fund investments to hire new staff, similar numbers of investments were dedicated to hiring staff to provide students social-emotional, behavioral, and/or mental support services (29 percent), support EL students (28 percent), and provide academic support in the form of instructional coaches, interventionists, and academic-focused administrators (23 percent), as shown in Table 4.3. Among staff classified as providing social-emotional, behavioral, and mental support, social workers, counselors, and psychologists were most common, constituting 19 percent of Opportunity Fund staff investments overall. Another popular staff position in this category (6 percent overall) was staff to serve as liaisons between schools, families, and communities. EL-related staff typically included ESL-certified classroom teachers, EL coaches and program administrators, paraprofessionals specifically for EL classrooms, and translators. Lastly, most academic support staff proposed by LEAs in their Opportunity Fund applications were either generalists capable of working across multiple subjects or reading-specific interventionists. Eleven percent of staffing investments were for general, unspecified staffing roles or miscellaneous roles, such as a motivational speaker.

Unsurprisingly, the most commonly proposed types of new staff hires mirrored the most common types of PD proposed by LEAs, demonstrating a common emphasis in increasing staff capacity to support EL students and students' social, emotional, behavioral, and mental health needs either through the hiring new staff or training existing staff.

Table 4.3. Categories of Proposed New Staff Hires with Opportunity Fund, Flexible Funds (n = 100)

Staff Type	Percentage	n
Social, behavioral, and mental support	29	29
Social worker, counselor, psychologist	19	19
Family and community engagement	6	6
General or other	4	4
EL	28	28
ESL-certified classroom teachers	9	9
EL other academic support (e.g., EL coaches)	5	5
EL paraprofessionals	3	3
EL translator	3	3
EL social, behavioral, and mental support	2	2
EL general or other	6	6
Academic support	23	23
Reading (e.g., specialist, interventionist, coach)	9	9
Math (e.g., specialist, interventionist, coach)	3	3
General or other	11	11
Paraprofessionals	9	9
Unspecified or other general hiring	11	11

SOURCE: LEA flexible Opportunity Funding applications provided to the authors.
NOTES: One hundred out of the 185 total proposed investments for Opportunity Funding flexible fund uses were to hire new staff.

Opportunity Funding—Mental Health and Reading Interventionist Investments

A total of 44 out of 45 schools that applied for the Mental Health and Reading Interventionist–specific stream of the Opportunity Fund received it.[14] Almost half (19 of 44) of these awards included funds to support both mental health and reading interventionist staff, followed by 12 and ten applications that requested and received funds for only mental health staff or reading interventionist staff, respectively (see Figure 4.5). The mental health staff that

[14] LEAs apply on behalf of their schools for these funds, listing planned investments by school. A total of 40 LEAs applied for these funds for one or more of their schools.

schools requested included school counselors, social and emotional specialists, therapists, school psychologists, social workers, and licensed professional counselors of mental health.

Figure 4.5. Types of Staff Requested via the Opportunity Fund Mental Health/Reading Interventionist Program in Fiscal Year 2020

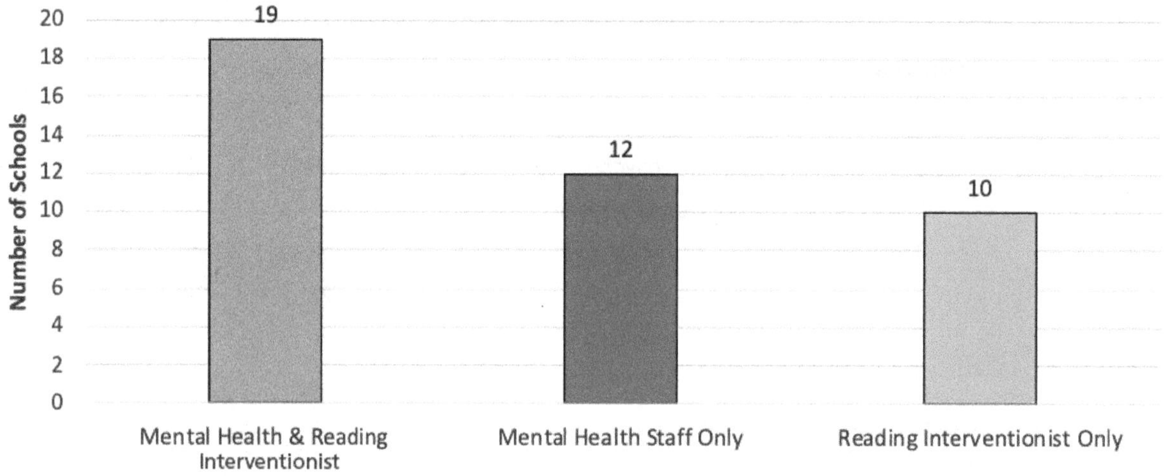

SOURCE: DDOE tracking file of mental health Opportunity Fund applications provided to the authors.
NOTE: Primary use of funds was missing for three of 44 schools that received mental health Opportunity Funds.

Student Success Block Grants—Special Education

Whereas all but one of the 41 LEAs in Delaware applied for the flexible Opportunity Funds or the mental health Opportunity Funds in the 2019–2020 school year, only two-thirds of LEAs qualified for either K–3 SPED or reading interventionist SSBG funding. Both funding streams of this program focus specifically on elementary grades, which explains why some LEAs (14, as shown in Table A.2) did not receive these funds. Nine of these 14 LEAs are charter schools, and one is a traditional school district (Delmar School District) that only serves middle and high school–aged students. Only two nonparticipating LEAs, Caesar Rodney and Woodbridge School District, were traditional public school districts that served students in grades K–12.

Similar to the Opportunity Fund program, LEAs primarily used SSBG SPED funds for hiring new staff and/or training of existing staff, according to our April 2020 survey of LEA leaders. Half of the 37 respondents indicated using SSBG funds to hire additional staff to serve SPED students, and 21 percent used these funds for training and PD for teachers, as shown in Table 4.4. Investments in curriculum (16 percent of LEAs) and classroom materials and supplies (11 percent) were the next most common uses of SSBG SPED funds.

Table 4.4. SSBG Special Education Investments, 2019–2020 (n = 37)

Category	Percentage	n
Staff	51	19
PD	22	8
Curriculum	16	6
Supplies	11	4
Programming	5	2
Other	13	5

SOURCE: April 2020 LEA survey.
NOTE: Use of SSBG funds was missing for three of 40 LEAs participating in the Opportunity Fund or SSBG.

Student Success Block Grants—Reading Interventionists

Using school-level demographic data from 2018–2019, the DDOE identified 45 eligible schools serving grades K–4 and meeting or exceeding the 2018–2019 enrollment thresholds of 60 percent LI students and/or 20 percent EL students in the 2018–2019 or 2017–2018 school years. Of these 45 eligible schools, DDOE records indicate that all 45 hired a reading interventionist in the 2019–2020 school year. In total, 15 LEAs contained at least one school that hired one of the 45 reading interventionists through the use of SSBG funds. In the April 2020 RAND survey, LEA leaders reported that SSBG-funded reading interventionists typically acted in supporting roles to lead classroom teachers, serving as pull-out teachers, interventionists, or instructional coaches. The 33 out of 45 interventionists who completed the DDOE's winter 2020 survey indicated a high degree of familiarity with numerous methods of reading instruction and content areas. They also had prevailingly high levels of experience and training, as summarized in the previous section about SSBG reading interventionist expenditures.

Implementation Status of Investments

Related to the last portion of the second research question, we summarize LEA's self-reported implementation efforts and barriers to implementation of their Opportunity Fund investments. In the April 2020 survey, we asked LEA leaders to indicate the status of their 2019–2020 Opportunity Fund investments at the midpoint of the academic year. Of the 185 Opportunity Fund investments proposed by LEAs, LEAs reported fully enacting 71 percent of them, partially enacting 6 percent, not enacting 6 percent of investments but still planning to in the remaining part of the 2019–2020 school year, and trying but being unable to implement 2 percent of investments; LEA leaders did not provide mid-year updates on 25 of the original 185 investments they had proposed in their applications and explicitly indicated that three of 185 investments were no longer relevant. Overall, traditional and charter LEAs did not appear to significantly differ in the implementation status of their Opportunity Fund investments.

Figure 4.6 shows the implementation status of the proposed Opportunity Fund investments by investment type. The two types of investments that were least likely to be fully implemented were additional programming (e.g., student and family programming) and PD, with staff investments the most likely to be fully implemented. This may be because of the timing of those investments was such that they had been delayed or else planned to occur in late spring or summer 2020.

Figure 4.6. Implementation Status of Opportunity Fund Flexible Fund Investments, by Investment Type (*n* = 185)

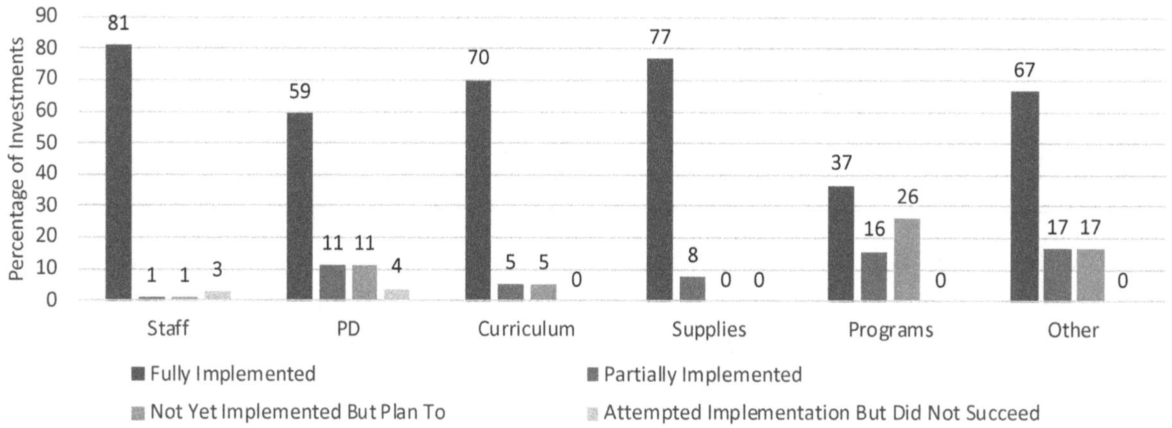

SOURCE: April 2020 LEA survey.

NOTES: Implementation status of Opportunity Fund investments was missing for 25 of the 185 investments. Percentages include these investments missing responses in the denominator.

Barriers to Implementation of the Opportunity Fund Investments

In the April 2020 RAND survey, we provided LEA leaders with a list of potential barriers to implementation and asked them to indicate, by investment, if they experienced any of these barriers, or another unlisted barrier, when attempting to implement a particular investment. We also offered an "other" category to allow the LEA leader respondent to indicate a barrier not already listed. We created the list of potential barriers from a prior survey of Delaware LEAs participating in the Opportunity Grants program in 2018 conducted by Klein, Mead, and Shapiro (2019) and sought DDOE input to further adjust the list based on their awareness of barriers.

Of the 185 Opportunity Fund investments, LEA leaders reported at least one type of barrier for 51 (about 28 percent) of these investments. They did not answer this question for 33 (18 percent) of the investments. We did not find that patterns of nonresponse differed between traditional and charter LEAs, nor were there significant demographic differences in the student composition of responding and nonresponding LEAs. Figure 4.7 shows the percentage of investments in a given investment type (e.g., staff, programming) for which barriers were reported. LEA leaders were most likely to report barriers in implementation for investments to implement new programming (42 percent of new programming investments), followed by purchasing supplies (31 percent) and providing staff PD (30 percent). This comports for the most part with the categories for which LEA leaders had reported implementation delays (shown in Figure 4.6). LEA leaders also reported barriers to implementation for three of the six total investments that we classified as "other"—e.g., providing transportation subsidies. LEA leaders were least likely to report investing in staff as encountering barriers (23 percent).

Figure 4.7. Percentage of Opportunity Fund Investments for which LEA Leaders Indicated There Were Barriers to Implementation, by Investment Type (*n* = 185)

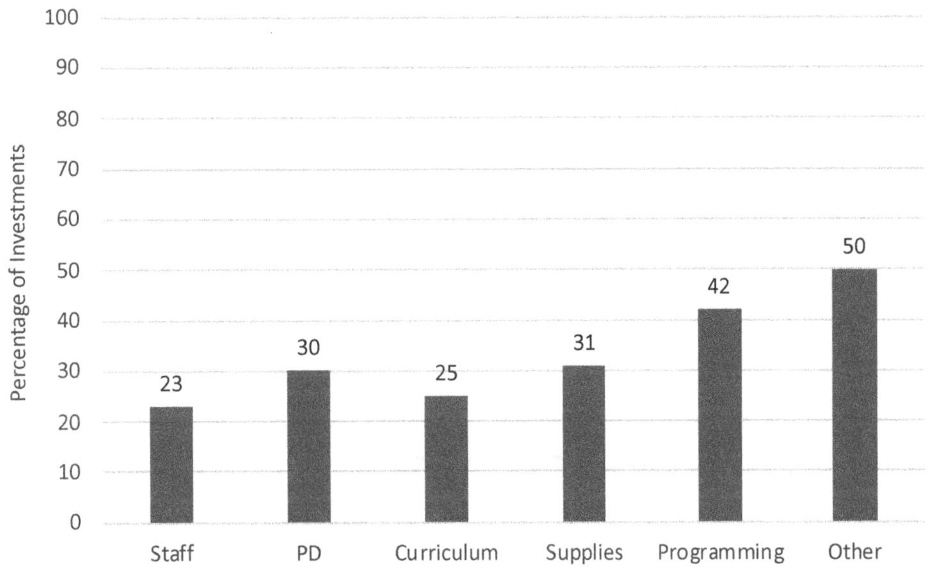

SOURCE: April 2020 LEA survey.
NOTES: Barriers to implementation were missing for 33 of 185 Opportunity Fund investments. Percentages include these investments missing responses in the denominator.

Because LEAs proposed, on average, four or five different Opportunity Fund investments during the 2019–2020 school year, 20 of 35 the LEA leaders who responded to our survey reported at least one type of barrier to implementing the investments. When examining the specific types of barriers that LEA leaders reported, having insufficient time to implement each investment was the most commonly cited barrier for both programming investments—where 27 percent of programming investments were cited to have faced this barrier—and PD investments (23 percent). Unsurprisingly, the inability to find qualified staff was the most frequently cited barrier for staff investments (22 percent), although it should be noted that LEAs reported that 20 percent of programming investments were also hindered inability to hire staff. Although we classify LEAs' investments based strictly on what is described in their applications, the prevalence of staff-based barriers for investments that are not classified as staff investments emphasizes that quality staff are often an essential and integral condition for the enactment of other types of investments. For curriculum investments, insufficient training (13 percent) was the most commonly cited barrier.

COVID-19 Adaptions to the Opportunity Fund and SSBG Investments

To answer our third research question about COVID-19 adaptations, we draw on LEA leaders' responses to DDOE's question in the summative conference and on the prework survey asking LEA leaders whether they were able to continue using their Opportunity Fund and SSBG investments following the transition to remote learning. Because staffing was the most common use of Opportunity Fund and SSBG funds, the vast majority of LEA leaders indicated that no change to their investments had occurred because these monies had already been committed to staff, and these staff remained employed. In the summative conferences that the DDOE held with 37 LEA leaders, 24 leaders reported being able to continue to use their Opportunity Fund monies, 15 said they were able to continue their SSBG reading interventionist funds, and 17 indicated using their SPED SSBG funding. (Recall that not all LEAs received SSBG funding, so less would report its continued usage.) Most LEAs also reported that they were able to continue using the interventions as intended. Districts that had SEL investments, such as Christina School District, reportedly put a priority on social-emotional well-being and learning during remote instruction.

However, some LEA leaders indicated that staff shifted their work as needed to provide remote instruction or support services. LEA leaders indicated that they were using Opportunity Fund and SSBG investments in creative ways to better support students during the remote learning period. For example, Kuumba Academy continued to use its investments for mental health services (which guidance counselors and the Dean of Culture and Behavior Interventionist provided), but these staff modified the methods they used to support students. They used online resources, such as newly offering virtual "home visits" with students and parents that comply with Centers for Disease Control and Prevention guidelines to mitigate risk of coronavirus infection, to modify their previous engagements. The staff also continued the weekly and biweekly meetings of the student support teams for at-risk and struggling students to organize their support services during COVID-19. Milford School District also used its staff to shift their outreach to students and families to become virtual. The Milford superintendent cited that the versatility of the staff was instrumental in providing the needed support for vulnerable populations. Their services included delivering meals to students and families, helping with transportation, providing cleaning supplies, helping families access medical assistance, assisting families with access to remote learning materials, and providing mental health checks. In addition, Milford School District used its summer program funding to continue providing these supports for its students and families after the 2019–2020 school year. The school leaders from this district modified their tutor position from full-time to half-time as teachers took over a greater role in the tutoring of students to maintain during remote learning the relationships they had built with students during in-person schooling.

One of Smyrna School District's adaptations during the spring 2020 remote learning period included providing online after-school tutoring and summer reading programming. Staff used Opportunity Fund dollars to purchase the American Reading Company online library and materials for staff, which allowed the LEA to continue providing resources in the online context. They also created a reading challenge for the summer in which the 2,000 students who completed the challenge were given ice cream gift certificates. Cape Henlopen School District also reallocated funds to provide greater online access for its students, reaching a near one-to-one relation of laptop/iPad-to-students across grades K–12.

LEA Leaders' Perceived Best Practices

To answer our final research question, we report on what LEA leaders felt were the most effective Opportunity Fund and SSBG investments. During their summative conferences and on the prework survey, LEA leaders indicated which Opportunity Fund and SSBG investments were most effective for improving the academic performance of LI, EL, and SPED students. Because Delaware canceled spring 2020 summative assessments in response to COVID-19, there were no statewide recent assessment data on which superintendents could draw. We are not certain, therefore, which assessment data (e.g., spring 2019, more-recent benchmark, or diagnostic assessments), if any, LEA leaders were drawing on in their answers. This is a limitation of this summary of their responses. LEAs were not restricted to selecting a single "most effective" investment, and, in practice, the vast majority of LEAs indicated several investments as among their most effective for a particular student group.

In Figure 4.8, we present the percentage of LEAs indicating that an investment in this category was among their most effective investments for raising the achievement of LI students (green), EL students (blue), and SPED students (yellow). The percentages presented in Figure 4.8, importantly, are calculated only among LEAs that reported using that type of investment.

Figure 4.8. Percentage of LEAs Indicating Investment Was "Most Effective" for Improving Student Academic Outcomes, by Type of Investment and Type of Student (n = 40)

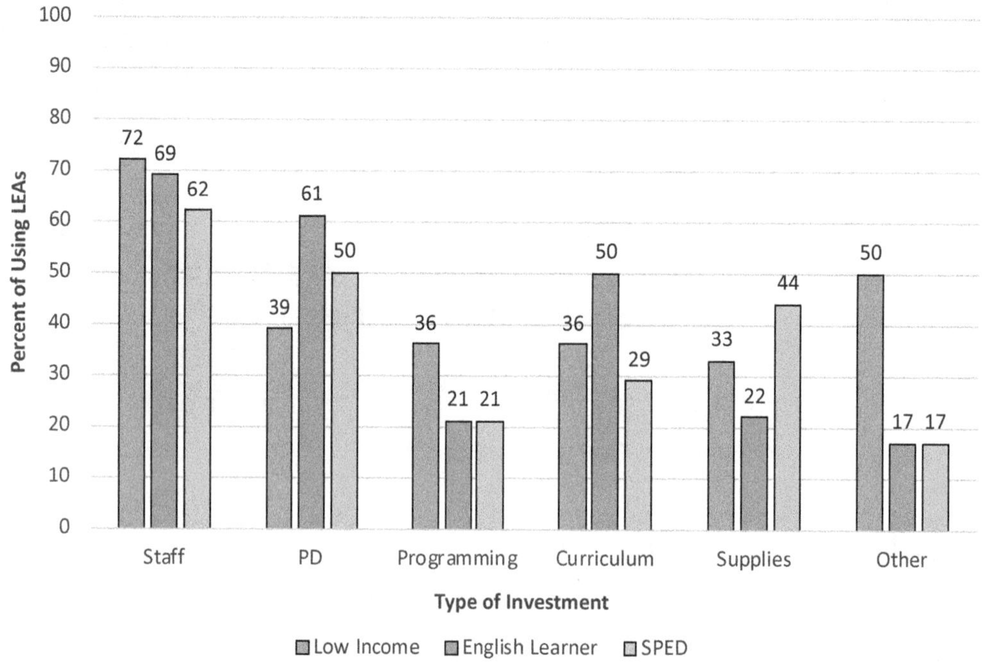

SOURCE: Summative LEA survey/conference.
NOTES: Percentages are calculated only among LEAs using that type of investment. LEAs referenced a total of 107 investments as being among their "most effective" for a particular type of student, with the most popular being staff investments (n = 37) to other (n = 8).

For each student subgroup, hiring new staff was reported to be the most effective investment by the largest proportion of LEAs: 72 percent for LI students, 69 percent for EL students, and 62 percent of SPED students. Within the broad category of staff investments, LEAs frequently indicated that social-emotional, behavioral, and mental health support staff (e.g., licensed clinical social workers and student behavior specialists) were one of their most important staff investments for these student subgroups. In particular, roughly 15 percent of LEA leaders mentioned the importance of staff members who assisted in building links between schools, families, and external resources to provide underserved students with coordinated supports for their well-being. Meanwhile, several LEA leaders, including those from Brandywine, First State Montessori, Las Americas ASPIRA Academy, and Seaford School Districts, mentioned the importance of teachers or administrators whose roles, such as a climate specialist, or a climate and culture dean, were dedicated toward developing school climate and culture in support of the performance of their students.

With regard to supporting LI students, LEAs were relatively balanced across the remaining types of investments, with 33 (supplies) to 50 percent (other) of LEAs using one of these investments, indicating that they were most effective. For EL students, LEAs reported that teacher PD and curriculum were the most effective investments after hiring new staff (61 percent and 50 percent, respectively). PD and classroom supply investments were most commonly reported as the most effective investments for SPED students, following hiring new staff.

5. Summary and Recommendations

The Opportunity Fund and SSBG programs comprised small shares of Delaware public schools' overall spending. The Opportunity Fund was, at most, 5 percent of any LEA's overall spending in 2019–2020, while the SSBG funding was, at most, 2 percent. However, the recent court settlement promises to triple Opportunity Funds by 2024–2025. Given this future expansion, it is all the more important to assess how LEAs expended the funds in the first year of these programs as a weighted pupil funding source. Early lessons can help inform subsequent year administration and design of the programs to improve their equity and effectiveness. For ease of reference, we organize the findings by program in the remainder of this chapter.

We reemphasize that the depth of our findings about implementation are limited by the brevity of surveys we fielded to LEA leaders. Interviews and case studies in the next two years of the evaluation should provide greater depth of information about the reasons for barriers and the expenditures.

Findings About the Flexible Opportunity Fund Program

- A large body of research indicates that increasing school funding generally leads to improvements in student educational outcomes, with larger effects for disadvantaged students. But not all programs that increased spending have yielded improvements in student achievement. Changes in instructional spending, such as those that result in reduced class sizes, the hiring of additional staff, additional staff compensation, and increased instructional time for students, appear most strongly associated with outcomes in which funding designs that allow LEAs flexibility within broad guidelines appear to be the most effective.
- Nearly all (40 out of the state's 41) LEAs participated in the flexible Opportunity Fund program, indicating near-universal participation across the state.
- LEAs expended almost $15 million out of the $20 million allocated for flexible Opportunity Funds in 2019–2020, leaving about 25 percent for future spending. Among the two-thirds of participating LEAs that did not fully expend their funds, they had an average of $216,859 of unspent funding at the end of 2019–2020 to roll over to future years. Charter school LEAs spent a greater share of their allocation than did traditional public school districts, which also meant they typically expended more flexible Opportunity Funds per pupil than did traditional public schools.
- Largely because LEAs often did not fully expend their allocations, per-pupil expenditures of flexible Opportunity Fund monies did not reach the targeted amounts of $300 per LI

student and $500 per EL student. The average expenditures across LEAs were $249 per LI and EL pupil in 2019–2020. Those LEAs that fully expended their allocations spent about $300 per EL and LI pupil, while those with remaining funds spent about $245 per LI and EL pupil.

- **Hiring new staff was by far the most common proposed investment LEAs made with flexible Opportunity Fund dollars.** Of the proposed new staff hires, about one-quarter were for staff to provide SEL or mental health support, one-quarter were for EL-related staff, and one-quarter were for other academic support, such as coaches and interventionists.
- New staff hires and the purchase of supplies were largely implemented as intended, while programming, such as summer camps and family engagement activities, were the least likely to have been fully implemented. Forty percent of planned new programs, 25 percent of planned PD for staff, 10 percent of planned curricula implementation, 8 percent of planned supply purchases, and 5 percent of planned new hires either partially occurred or had not occurred in April 2020 when we surveyed LEA leaders. One possible reason of this could be the timing of the survey; several of the unfinished investments were planned to occur in spring or summer 2020 after the survey was administered. Another could be delays caused by COVID-19.
- The types of investments with the most barriers reported by LEA leaders were new programming, PD, and supply investments, echoing LEA leaders' responses regarding implementation status. As to be expected, the investments with the most reported barriers were also generally the ones that had not yet been or were only partially implemented.
- Across the board, more school staff was the type of investment LEA leaders endorsed as most effective for improving academic outcomes for all three of the EL, LI, and SPED student subgroups. LEA leaders especially called out the importance of staff supporting student mental, social, and behavioral well-being. Beyond the general endorsement of more staff, there were some differences in LEA leaders' responses for particular student groups. For EL, LEA chiefs endorsed the following three categories as most effective in descending order: more staff (62 percent of LEA leaders), PD (61 percent), and EL curriculum (50 percent). For SPED students, LEA leaders identified the following as top three: more staff (62 percent of LEA leaders), PD (50 percent), and supplies (44 percent). For LI students, LEA leaders identified the following as the top three: more staff (72 percent); other investments, such as bookmobiles and the use of academic screeners (50 percent); and PD (39 percent). PD was consistently ranked among the top three most effective uses, as did the importance of resources specific to a student subgroup (such as curricular materials for ELs or supportive classroom materials and supplies for SPED students).

- Most LEAs continued to use their flexible Opportunity Fund investments for staff during COVID-19 but adjusted staff activities to provide services remotely. For example, certain LEAs extending the role of school-family liaisons to include such responsibilities as meal delivery and remote mental health check-ins and using funding to provide laptops and tablets to students.

Findings About the Mental Health Opportunity Fund Program

- Prior research about mental health services in elementary schools suggests that increasing students' access to school counselors and/or social workers can result in modest increases in student achievement, with more robust evidence of impacts on student disciplinary and behavioral outcomes.
- Forty-four schools in 15 LEAs used mental health Opportunity Funds. They did so for staff hires, such as social workers, licensed professional counselors of mental health, school psychologists, and reading interventionists. These 44 schools expended, on average, $91,320 per school in 2019–2020. This program was the only one out of the four that did not allocate funds based on student enrollment counts. Instead, LEAs submitted applications to the DDOE for investments in qualifying schools.
- The design of this particular program created greater inequity in the allocation amounts across schools than did the other three programs. Whereas the SSBG reading interventionist program allocated up to one FTE staff per qualifying school, and the flexible Opportunity Fund and SSBG SPED dollars were allocated based on counts of qualifying pupils, the mental health Opportunity Fund allocations were driven by LEA applications for qualifying schools. In the 44 applications for mental health funding, the number of requested investments per qualifying school ranged from one to six, and the requested amount ranged from $46,956 to $257,784.
- Consistent with the variability in requested amounts, expenditures varied by a factor of six, ranging from as little as $23,553 to as much as $159,777 per qualifying school in 2019–2020. Charter LEAs were the most likely to spend the greatest amount of mental health Opportunity Funds per school.
- LEAs expended almost $3.5 million out of the $5 million allocated for mental health Opportunity Funds in 2019–2020, leaving about 30 percent for future spending. This was the largest percentage of unspent funds among the four programs. LEAs that did not fully expend their funds (which was about two-thirds of participating LEAs and included charter and traditional LEAs equally) had an average of $216,859 of unspent funding at the end of 2019–2020 to roll over to the next year.
- Staffing shortages may be the reason the mental health program had the greatest share of unspent funds by the end of the 2019–2020 school year. This program focused on hiring

staff for positions where there was the greatest shortage of certificated individuals for elementary schools—i.e., social workers and psychologists. Virtually all individuals who held Delaware certification for school psychologists, school social workers, and bilingual certificated individuals were employed in a Delaware public school in 2019–2020. This contrasts with other certificate types, where there are several hundred or more Delaware certificated individuals who are not employed by the Delaware public schools: SPED teachers, paraprofessionals, counselors, reading interventionists, and teachers of ELs.

Findings About the SSBG Special Education Grants

- Among the most effective investments for SPED students in elementary grades are increased supports for developing teachers' instructional, behavioral, and socio-emotional capacity when working with these students. Teacher focus on PBIS, direct student instruction, and development of student strategies were among the most effective interventions for supporting SPED students. PD interventions for SPED teachers were most effective when they incorporated performance feedback and modeling of specific strategies.
- Twenty-seven of the state's 42 LEAs expended these funds in 2019–2020. The elementary grade–focus of both SSBG funding streams explains the 36 percent nonparticipation rate; most of the LEAs that did not participate were charter schools that serve only middle or high school grades.
- LEAs expended about $3.4 million out of the approximately $4.5 million allocated for SSBG SPED grants, leaving about 25 percent for future spending. Charter LEAs had higher per-pupil expenditures than traditional public schools, with a few exceptions, reflecting the fact that they were also the LEAs with the least amount of unexpended funds. Of the 17 out of 27 LEAs that did not fully expend their allocation in 2019–2020, they typically left $103,293 unspent.
- The highest-spending LEA ($1,118 of SSBG SPED monies per K–3 SPED enrollee) spent seven times more than the lowest-spending LEA ($147 of SSBG SPED monies per K–3 SPED enrollee). Although funds were allocated on a per-pupil basis, which equitably allocates funds, the high degree of variation in per-pupil expenditure stemmed primarily from the degree to which LEAs expended their allocations.
- The main investment that LEAs made with these funds was the hire of additional staff to serve SPED students. The next most-common uses were for PD for teachers, curriculum purchases, and supplies.
- Similar to flexible Opportunity Fund investments, because most SSBG funds were used toward hiring new staff, these investments continued to be used during the remote learning period of spring 2020. We do not have an indication from LEA leaders'

summative conference responses how, if at all, they adapted SSBG-hired staff activities during COVID-19.

Findings About the SSBG Reading Interventionists

- Prior research about reading interventionists points to beneficial effects through both interventionists providing direct instruction to students and coaching of other staff. Students participating in reading interventions saw modest to medium improvements of 0.1–0.3 standard deviations on reading assessments. Teachers undergoing coaching from a reading or literacy coach typically see larger increases of 0.5 standard deviations on measures of classroom instruction.
- LEAs expended almost all of the $3.97 million allocated for the SSBG reading interventionist program. Three percent of the 2019–2020 allocation is available for future spending.
- All 45 qualifying schools across 15 LEAs hired an SSBG-funded reading interventionist. Funding covered the full-time hire of up to one reading interventionist per school at the 45 qualifying schools.
- The average per-school expenditure in the 15 LEAs on reading interventionists ranged from $41,331 to $119,165. Differences in expenditures reflected the variation in experience and qualification levels and LEA pay scales and possibly also the half-time versus full-time status of the 45 interventionists.
- We are not aware of COVID-19 adaptations specific to reading interventionist staff roles and duties.

Recommendations

Drawing on these findings, we offer several recommendations. We expect to refine and extend these recommendations in future reports as we examine trends in spending and investments and labor market responses over the three-year span of the evaluation.

- The DDOE should work with LEAs to identify barriers to implementing investments to fully expend their allocations in ways that benefit student achievement—particularly in those LEAs that are leaving the largest share of the funds unspent. These are often the same LEAs across several of the four programs.
- Because of a program design that leaves room for greater variability in per-school allocations, the DDOE should revisit the mental health Opportunity Fund program to ensure that those funds are equitably distributed.
- The DDOE should investigate LEAs' barriers to expending the SSBG SPED funding, given that many investments were focused on hiring staff, and there is no shortage of

certificated SPED teachers in Delaware. Also, LEA leaders reported that the purchase of supplies was an effective investment for SPED services in particular, yet LEAs were relatively infrequently listing these investments in their applications.

- Delaware certification programs should seek to expand recruitment of candidates for social workers, school psychologists, and other shorthanded certifications fields, given LEA leaders' perceptions of the effectiveness of these services and the likely continued focus on mental health and SEL services, especially in the wake of COVID-19.

Focus of RAND's Future Reports

Finally, this report raises several new questions that we intend to investigate in future reports. In addition to updated accounting of Opportunity Fund and SSBG investments, analyses of their effects on student achievement, and best practices, we intend to answer the following questions:

- Are there internal staffing shifts that are not reflected in overall shortages of categories of certificated staff? For example, is there an internal shift of classroom teachers to reading interventionists, or vice versa, that might alter schools' approach to reading instruction?
- What are the main reasons LEAs are leaving allocated funds unspent?
- What processes and resources does Delaware use to recruit applicants for certification program training? Are there ways to target more intensively applicants for high-need certifications?
- Are LEAs replacing a portion of their local contributions to school spending with the additional state funding from the Opportunity Fund or SSBG programs?
- Do LEAs favor one program over another among the four weighted pupil funding programs? If so, why?
- What creative ways are LEAs using flexible Opportunity Funds in particular?

Appendix. Supplemental Data Tables

This appendix provides supplemental data referenced in the body of the report.

Table A.1. Demographic Characteristics of Delaware LEAs That Participated in the Opportunity Fund or SSBG in the 2019–2020 School Year

						Student Characteristics (Percentage)				
LEA Name	Urbanicity	LEA Type	Number of Schools	Number of High-Need Schools	Total Enrollment	LI	EL	SWD	Black	Hispanic
Academia Antonia Alonso	Suburban	Charter	1	1	632	49.7	55.4	11.6	16.6	73.7
Academy of Dover Charter School	City	Charter	1	0	295	57.6	9.2	12.9	78.6	10.5
Appoquinimink School District	Town	Traditional	17	0	12,489	13.1	3.6	18.9	27.7	8.3
Brandywine School District	Suburban	Traditional	17	1	11,826	30.3	5.8	20.1	39.0	7.6
Caesar Rodney School District	Suburban	Traditional	13	0	8,680	28.9	4.7	19.6	26.9	9.2
Campus Community School	City	Traditional	1	0	425	41.2	4.2	14.1	56.2	8.9
Cape Henlopen School District	Town	Traditional	9	1	6,122	25.8	8.6	21.5	11.8	15.8
Capital School District	City	Traditional	13	2	7,425	48.0	7.9	24.6	52.4	13.3
Charter School of New Castle	Suburban	Traditional	1	0	811	47.2	3.0	13.4	84.7	8.1
Charter School of Wilmington	City	Charter	1	0	976	4.3		0.8	7.7	5.8
Christina School District	Suburban	Traditional	28	8	15,918	40.8	13.7	25.0	40.7	21.6
Colonial School District	Suburban	Traditional	15	5	10,971	38.0	12.7	22.6	45.5	21.2
Delmar School District	Suburban	Traditional	2	0	1,491	15.6	4.2	11.3	15.6	10.7
Early College High School at Del State	City	Charter	1	0	445	33.3		7.2	75.1	10.8
East Side Charter School	City	Charter	1	1	476	77.5		16.8	93.7	4.4
Edison (Thomas A.) Charter School	City	Charter	1	1	771	76.3	0.8	11.5	97.0	1.2
First State Military Academy	Rural	Charter	1	0	461	20.2	1.5	16.7	28.2	13.2
First State Montessori Academy	City	Charter	1	0	611	10.8	1.2	14.7	16.7	2.8
Freire Charter School Wilmington	City	Charter	1	0	565	44.3	2.7	21.1	75.2	11.5
Gateway Lab School	Suburban	Charter	1	0	185	43.2	4.9	52.4	53.5	11.4
Great Oaks Charter School	City	Charter	1	1	520	62.5	5.4	24.2	81.2	12.5
Indian River School District	Town	Traditional	15	6	11,340	29.5	23.3	18.0	11.3	37.1

LEA Name	Urbanicity	LEA Type	Number of Schools	Number of High-Need Schools	Total Enrollment	Student Characteristics (Percentage)				
						LI	EL	SWD	Black	Hispanic
Kuumba Academy Charter School	City	Charter	1	1	690	62.2	1.3	19.9	91.0	5.5
Lake Forest School District	Rural	Traditional	7	1	3,963	38.7	2.6	22.5	23.3	8.3
Las Americas Aspira Academy	Suburban	Charter	1	1	964	26.8	35.1	14.1	12.7	66.1
Laurel School District	Suburban	Traditional	4	1	2,924	45.3	14.6	19.3	26.3	17.2
MOT Charter School	Rural	Charter	1	0	1,392	6.7	2.0	8.3	24.5	7.5
Milford School District	Town	Traditional	6	1	4,608	40.4	18.0	19.1	25.2	21.4
New Castle County Vo-Tech School District	Suburban	VoTech	4	0	4,724	27.5	3.6	13.8	39.3	26.7
Newark Charter School	Suburban	Charter	1	0	2,417	9.0	3.5	9.1	11.6	
Odyssey Charter School	Suburban	Charter	1	0	1,927	13.6	4.3	11.1	23.3	7.6
Polytech School District	Rural	VoTech	1	0	1,214	20.0		10.2	21.8	8.4
Positive Outcomes Charter School	Suburban	Charter	1	0	125	37.6		64.8	37.6	8.8
Providence Creek Academy Charter School	Rural	Charter	1	0	709	18.1	1.7	13.1	23.7	4.9
Red Clay Consolidated School District	Suburban	Traditional	28	12	18,187	31.7	15.1	19.5	21.6	27.4
Seaford School District	Suburban	Traditional	6	4	3,801	46.1	20.3	20.1	36.3	22.9
Smyrna School District	Rural	Traditional	8	0	6,204	25.2	2.5	20.5	30.5	8.3
Sussex Academy	Town	Charter	1	0	876	8.7	1.9	4.7	4.1	14.3
Sussex Technical School District	Rural	VoTech	1	0	1,258	20.0	1.0	9.2	14.5	14.8
Woodbridge School District	Town	Traditional	4	0	2,833	42.2	14.8	19.5	21.6	24.8
Delaware Public Schools	-	-	219	48	147,557	31.3	10.4	19.4	30.7	18.2

SOURCES: Delaware Open Data, 2020b; NCES Common Core of Data 2018–2019 (Urbanicity).
NOTES: A *high-need school* is determined using the guidelines to determine eligibility for mental health/reading interventionist grant under the Opportunity Fund program and is defined as a school whose enrollments consist of either 60 percent LI students and or 20 percent EL students. Blank cells are because of small sample size censoring.

Table A.2. Delaware LEAs Expenditures in Fiscal Year 2020

LEA Name	Total Expenditures	Total Expenditures per Pupil	Opportunity Fund, Flexible Fund	Opportunity Fund, Mental Health	SSBG, Special Education	SSBG, Reading Interventionists
Academia Antonia Alonso	$8,437,555	$13,351	$243,473	$148,403	$52,590	$41,332
Academy of Dover Charter School	$3,465,820	$11,749	$101,441	$63,658	$3,838	$80,424
Appoquinimink School District	$237,658,432	$19,029	$393,355		$428,789	
Brandywine School District	$218,177,424	$18,449	$932,246	$70,276	$527,747	$71,178
Caesar Rodney School District	$143,229,664	$16,501	$412,781			
Campus Community School	$4,698,922	$11,056	$49,900		$12,903	
Cape Henlopen School District	$163,337,040	$26,680	$379,178	$74,651	$199,331	$96,688
Capital School District	$122,011,280	$16,432	$819,505	$100,244	$214,801	$139,858
Charter School of New Castle	$10,269,136	$12,662	$98,673		$27,817	
Charter School of Wilmington	$10,619,541	$10,881	$11,900			
Christina School District	$243,597,728	$15,303	$1,343,983	$188,426	$201,821	$862,709
Colonial School District	$167,807,184	$15,296	$1,817,665	$581,010	$207,540	$595,825
Delmar School District	$16,338,457	$10,958	$78,037			
Early College High School	$4,560,674	$10,249	$39,854			
East Side Charter School	$7,237,709	$15,205	$78,156	$106,202	$18,545	$81,102
First State Military Academy	$5,925,039	$12,853	$30,600			
First State Montessori Academy	$8,219,167	$13,452	$16,899		$7,418	
Freire Charter School	$7,503,435	$13,280	$66,900			
Gateway Lab School	$4,802,824	$25,961	$24,000		$1,854	
Great Oaks Charter School	$7,899,302	$15,191	$77,939			
Indian River School District	$165,852,816	$14,625	$1,548,470	$453,174	$267,442	$313,966
Kuumba Academy Charter School	$10,757,851	$15,591	$136,851	$121,974	$48,217	$85,599
Lake Forest School District	$54,388,964	$13,724	$385,440		$110,160	

LEA Name	Total Expenditures	Total Expenditures per Pupil	Opportunity Fund, Flexible Fund	Opportunity Fund, Mental Health	SSBG, Special Education	SSBG, Reading Interventionists
Las Americas ASPIRA	$17,363,468	$18,012	$217,736	$159,777	$25,963	$81,102
Laurel School District	$35,179,432	$12,031	$323,909		$60,516	
Milford School District	$58,200,356	$12,630	$529,469	$105,714	$90,801	$97,841
MOT Charter School	$16,411,622	$11,790	$23,356		$29,305	
New Castle County Vo-Tech School	$105,487,744	$22,330	$343,798			
Newark Charter School	$34,948,496	$14,459	$103,800		$48,217	
Odyssey Charter	$27,912,272	$14,485	$93,735		$51,925	
Polytech School District	$24,839,586	$20,461	$63,300			
Positive Outcomes Charter School	$3,532,038	$28,256	$11,400			
Providence Creek Acad Charter School	$7,927,115	$11,181	$39,900		$24,108	
Red Clay Consolidated School District	$272,124,352	$14,963	$2,539,678	$856,977	$468,102	$841,606
Seaford School District	$50,966,920	$13,409	$471,137	$388,621	$64,969	$355,923
Smyrna School District	$82,391,888	$13,280	$389,367		$134,539	
Sussex Academy of Arts/Science	$9,790,076	$11,176	$28,500			
Sussex Technical School District	$25,672,670	$20,408	$65,800			
Thomas A. Edison Charter School	$9,655,856	$12,524	$248,727	$57,518	$34,934	$115,448
Woodbridge School District	$40,784,044	$14,396	$372,947			

SOURCE: FY 2020 validity file provided to the authors.

References

August, Diane, Lee Branum-Martin, Elsa Cardenas-Hagan, and David J. Francis, "The Impact of an Instructional Intervention on the Science and Language Learning of Middle Grade English Language Learners," *Journal of Research on Educational Effectiveness*, Vol. 2, No. 4, 2009, pp. 345–376.

August, Diane, and Timothy Shanahan, eds., Executive Summary: Developing Literacy in Second-Language Learners: Report of the National Literacy Panel on Language Minority Children and Youth, Mahwah, N.J., and London: Lawrence Erlbaum Associates, 2006.

Baron, E. Jason, *School Spending and Student Outcomes: Evidence from Revenue Limit Elections in Wisconsin*, October 24, 2019. As of December 23, 2020: https://childandfamilypolicy.duke.edu/wp-content/uploads/2020/12/Baron_Jason_TEEW_sm.pdf

Barrett, Susan B., Catherine P. Bradshaw, and Teri Lewis-Palmer, "Maryland Statewide PBIS Initiative: Systems, Evaluation, and Next Steps," *Journal of Positive Behavior Interventions*, Vol. 10, No. 2, April 2008, pp. 105–114.

Benner, Gregory J., Kathleen M. Beaudoin, Pei-Yu Chen, Carol Davis, and Nicole C. Ralston, "The Impact of Intensive Positive Behavioral Supports on the Behavior Functional of Students with Emotional Disturbance: How Much Does Fidelity Matter?" *Journal of Assessment and Intervention in Children*, Vol. 1, No. 1, 2010, pp. 85–100.

Bitler, Marianne P., and Lynn A. Karoly, "Intended and Unintended Effects of the War on Poverty: What Research Tells Us and Implications for Policy," *Journal of Policy Analysis and Management*, Vol. 34, No. 3, 2015, pp. 639–696.

Bowden, A. Brooks, Atsuko Belfield, Henry M. Levin, Robert Shand, Anyi Wang, and Melisa Morales, *A Benefit-Cost Analysis of City Connects*, New York: Teachers College, Columbia University, July 2015. As of December 14, 2020: https://static1.squarespace.com/static/583b86882e69cfc61c6c26dc/t/58cfdcba1b631bf52d377cd8/1490017468049/CityConnects.pdf

Bradshaw Catherine P., Mary M. Mitchell, and Phillip J. Leaf, "Examining the Effects of Schoolwide Positive Behavioral Interventions and Supports on Student Outcomes: Results from a Randomized Controlled Effectiveness Trail in Elementary Schools," *Journal of Positive Behavior Interventions*, Vol. 12, No. 3, 2010, pp. 133–148.

Brock, Matthew E., and Erik W. Carter, "A Meta-Analysis of Educator Training to Improve Implementation of Interventions for Students with Disabilities," *Remedial and Special Education*, Vol. 38, No. 3, 2017, pp. 131–144.

Bryant, Diane P., Sylvia Linan-Thompson, Nicole Ugel, Allison Hamff, and Marty Hougen, "The Effects of Professional Development for Middle School General and Special Education Teachers on Implementation of Reading Strategies in Inclusive Content Area Classes," *Learning Disability Quarterly*, Vol. 24, No. 4, 2001, pp. 251–264.

Candelaria, Christopher A., and Kenneth A. Shores, "Court-Ordered Finance Reforms in the Adequacy Era: Heterogeneous Causal Effects and Sensitivity," *Education Finance and Policy*, Vol. 14, No. 1, Winter 2019, pp. 31–60.

Carrell, Scott E., and Mark Hoekstra, "Are School Counselors an Effective Education Input?" *Economics Letters*, Vol. 125, No. 1, 2014, pp. 66–69.

Castleman, Benjamin, and Joshua Goodman, "Intensive College Counseling and the Enrollment and Persistence of Low-Income Students," *Education Finance and Policy*, Vol. 13, No. 1, Winter 2018, pp. 19–41.

Cellini, Stephanie Riegg, Fernando Ferreira, and Jesse Rothstein, "The Value of School Facility Investments: Evidence from a Dynamic Regression Discontinuity Design," *Quarterly Journal of Economics*, Vol. 125, No. 1, February 2010, pp. 215–261.

Chetty, Raj, John N. Friedman, Nathaniel Hilger, Emmanuel Saez, Diane Whitmore Schanzenbach, and Danny Yagan, "How Does Your Kindergarten Classroom Affect Your Earnings? Evidence from Project STAR," *Quarterly Journal of Economics*, Vol. 126, No. 4, November 2011, pp. 1593–1660.

Coleman, James S., Ernest Q. Campbell, Carol J. Hobson, James McPartland, Alexander M. Mood, Frederic D. Weinfeld, and Robert L. York, *Equality of Educational Opportunity*, Washington, D.C.: U.S. Government Printing Office, 1966.

Conlin, Michael and Paul N. Thompson, "Impacts of New School Facility Construction: An Analysis of a State-Financed Capital Subsidy Program in Ohio," *Economics of Education Review*, Vol. 59, 2017, pp. 13–28.

Delaware Open Data, "Educator Characteristics," data set, February 27, 2020a. As of December 15, 2020: https://data.delaware.gov/Education/Educator-Characteristics/t9ya-d7ak

Delaware Open Data, "Student Enrollment," data set, September 25, 2020b. As of December 15, 2020: https://data.delaware.gov/Education/Student-Enrollment/6i7v-xnmf

Durlak, Joseph A., Roger P. Weissberg, Allison B. Dymnicki, Rebecca D. Taylor, and Kriston B. Schellinger, "The Impact of Enhancing Students' Social and Emotional Learning: A Meta-Analysis of School-Based Universal Interventions," *Child Development*, Vol. 82, No. 1, February 2011, pp. 405–432.

Education Commission of the States, *The Progress of Education Reform: Understanding State School Funding*, Vol. 13, No. 3, June 2012. As of December 15, 2020: http://www.ecs.org/clearinghouse/01/02/86/10286.pdf

Fletcher, Jason, "Spillover Effects of Inclusion of Classmates with Emotional Problems on Test Scores in Early Elementary School," *Journal of Policy Analysis and Management*, Vol. 29, No. 1, Winter 2010, pp. 69–83.

Foley, Elizabeth, "Student-Based Budgeting in Tough Times: The New York City Experience," *Voices in Urban Education*, No. 29, 2010, pp. 6–16.

Gilraine, Michael, Hugh Macartney, and Robert McMillan, *Estimating the Direct and Indirect Effects of Major Education Reforms*, Cambridge, Mass.: National Bureau of Economic Research, January 2018, revised August 2020.

Goncalves, Felipe M., *The Effects of School Construction on Student and District Outcomes: Evidence from a State-Funded Program in Ohio,* Princeton, N.J.: Princeton University, working paper 593, 2015.

Gottfried, Michael A., Anna Egalite, and Jacob J. Kirksey, "Does the Presence of a Classmate with Emotional/Behavioral Disabilities Link to Other Students' Absences in Kindergarten?" *Early Childhood Research Quarterly*, Vol. 36, No. 3, 2016, pp. 506–520.

Gottfried, Michael A., and Aletha Harven, "Classmates with Emotional and Behavioral Disorders and the Proactive Nature of Peer Gender," *Journal of Educational Research*, Vol. 108, No. 1, 2015, pp. 45–61.

Hamilton, Laura S., Christopher Joseph Doss, and Elizabeth D. Steiner, *Teacher and Principal Perspectives on Social and Emotional Learning in America's Schools: Findings from the American Educator Panels*, Santa Monica, Calif.: RAND Corporation, RR-2991-BMGF, 2019. As of December 15, 2020: https://www.rand.org/pubs/research_reports/RR2991.html

Hanover Research, *A Meta-Analysis of Research on English Learners: Prepared for the Riverside County Office of Education*, Arlington, Va.: Hanover Researcher, 2015.

Hanushek, Eric A., "Throwing Money at Schools," *Journal of Policy Analysis and Management*, Vol. 1, No. 1, Autumn 1981, pp. 19–41.

Hanushek, Eric A., "The Economics of Schooling: Production and Efficiency in Public Schools," *Journal of Economic Literature*, Vol. 49, No. 3, September 1986, pp. 1141–1177.

Hanushek, Eric A., "The Failure of Input-Based Schooling Policies," *Economic Journal*, Vol. 113, No. 485, February 2003, pp. F64–98.

Hedges, Larry V., Richard D. Laine, and Rob Greenwald, "Does Money Matter? A Meta-Analysis of Studies of the Effects of Differential School Inputs on Student Outcomes," *Educational Researcher*, Vol. 23, No. 3, April 1994, pp. 5–14.

Henry, Gary T., C. Kevin Fortner, and Charles L. Thompson, "Targeted Funding for Educationally Disadvantaged Students: A Regression Discontinuity Estimate of the Impact on High School Student Achievement," *Educational Evaluation and Policy Analysis*, Vol. 32, No. 2, June 2010, pp. 183–204.

Hong, Kai, and Ron Zimmer, "Does Investing in School Capital Infrastructure Improve Student Achievement?" *Economics of Education Review*, Vol. 53, 2016, pp. 143–158.

Horner, Robert H., George M. Sugai, Keith Smolkowski, Lucille Eber, Jean Nakasto, Anne W. Todd, and Jody Esperanza, "A Randomized, Wait-List Controlled Effectiveness Trail Assessing School-Wide Positive Behavior Support in Elementary Schools," *Journal of Positive Behavior Interventions*, Vol. 11, No. 3, 2009, pp. 133–144.

Hurwitz, Michael, and Jessica Howell, *Measuring the Impact of High School Counselors on College Enrollment*, Washington, D.C.: College Board Advocacy & Policy Center, February 2013.

Ihlo, Tanya, and Melissa Nantais, "Evidence-Based Interventions Within a Multi-Tier Framework for Positive Behavioral Supports," in Todd A. Glover and Sharon Vaughn, eds., *The Promise of Response to Intervention: Evaluating Current Science and Practice*, New York: Guilford Publications, March 2010, pp. 239–266.

Jackson, C. Kirabo, *Does School Spending Matter? The New Literature on an Old Question*, Cambridge, Mass.: National Bureau of Economic Research, working paper 25368, December 2018.

Jackson, C. Kirabo, Rucker C. Johnson, and Claudia Persico, "The Effects of School Spending on Educational and Economic Outcomes: Evidence from School Finance Reforms," *Quarterly Journal of Economics*, Vol. 131, No. 1, 2016, pp. 157–218.

Jackson, C. Kirabo, Cora Wigger, and Heyu Xiong, *Do School Spending Cuts Matter? Evidence from the Great Recession*, Cambridge, Mass.: National Bureau of Economic Research, working paper 24203, January 2018, revised August 2019.

Jenkins, Amelia, and Jodi Yoshimura, "Meeting the Special Education Professional Development Needs of Elementary General Educators," *Teaching Exceptional Children*, Vol. 42, No. 5, 2010, pp. 36–43.

Jepsen, Christopher, and Steven Rivkin, "Class Size Reduction and Student Achievement: The Potential Tradeoff Between Teacher Quality and Class Size," *Journal of Human Resources*, Vol. 44, No. 1, Winter 2009, pp. 223–250.

Johnson, Rucker C., and Sean Tanner, *Money and Freedom: The Impact of California's School Finance Reform*, Palo Alto, Calif.: Getting Down to Facts, September 2018. As of December 15, 2020: https://learningpolicyinstitute.org/product/ca-school-finance-reform-brief

Klein, Jeff, Hilary Mead, and Alissa Shapiro, *2018/2019 School Year Opportunity Grant Analysis*, Newark, Del.: Center for Research in Education & Social Policy, University of Delaware, April 2019.

Kraft, Matthew A., David Blazar, and Dylan Hogan, "The Effect of Teacher Coaching on Instruction and Achievement: A Meta-Analysis of the Causal Evidence," *Review of Educational Research*, Vol. 88, No. 4, 2018, pp. 547–588.

LaFortune, Julien, Jesse Rothstein, and Diane Whitmore Schanzenbach, "School Finance Reform and the Distribution of Student Achievement," *American Economic Journal: Applied Economics*, Vol. 10, No. 2, April 2018, pp. 1–26.

Lee-St. John, Terrence J., Mary E. Walsh, Anastasia E. Raczek, Caroline E. Vuilleumier, Claire Foley, Amy Heberle, Erin Sibley, and Eric Dearing, "The Long-Term Impact of Systemic Student Support in Elementary School: Reducing High School Dropout," *AERA Open*, Vol. 4, No. 4, October–December 2018, pp. 1–16.

Leko, Melinda, and Mary T. Brownell, "Crafting Quality Professional Development for Special Educators: What School Leaders Should Know," *Teaching Exceptional Children*, Vol. 42, No. 1, September–October 2009, pp. 64–70.

Lesaux, Nonie K., Michael J. Kieffer, Joan G. Kelley, and Julie Russ Harris, "Effects of Academic Vocabulary Instruction for Linguistically Diverse Adolescents: Evidence from a Randomized Field Trial," *American Educational Research Journal*, Vol. 51, No. 6, December 2014, pp. 1159–1194.

Ludwig, Caralyn, Kan Guo, and George K. Georgiou, "Are Reading Interventions for English Language Learners Effective? A Meta-Analysis," *Journal of Learning Disabilities*, Vol. 52, No. 3, 2019, pp. 220–231.

Martorell, Paco, Kevin Stange, and Isaac McFarlin, Jr., "Investing in Schools: Capital Spending, Facility Conditions, and Student Achievement," *Journal of Public Economics*, Vol. 140, 2016, pp. 13–29.

Master, Benjamin, Susanna Loeb, Camille Whitney, and James Wyckoff, "Different Skills? Identifying Differentially Effective Teachers of English Language Learners," *Elementary School Journal*, Vol. 117, No. 2, 2016, pp. 261–283.

Matuchniak, Tina, Carol Booth Olson, and Robin Scarcella, "Examining the Text-Based, On-Demand, Analytical Writing of Mainstreamed Latino English Learners in a Randomized Field Trial of the Pathway Project Intervention," *Reading and Writing: An Interdisciplinary Journal*, Vol. 27, No. 6, July 2014, pp. 973–994.

Mulhern, Christine, *Beyond Teachers: Estimating Individual Guidance Counselors' Effects on Educational Attainment*, May 28, 2020. As of December 15, 2020: http://papers.cmulhern.com/Counselors_Mulhern.pdf

Polikoff, Morgan, Elaine Lin Wang, Shira Korn Haderlein, Julia H. Kaufman, Ashley Woo, Daniel Silver, and V. Darleen Opfer, *Exploring Coherence in English Language Arts Instructional Systems in the Common Core Era*, Santa Monica, Calif.: RAND Corporation, RR-A279-1, 2020. As of November 10, 2020: https://www.rand.org/pubs/research_reports/RRA279-1.html

Quatroche, Diana J., Rita M. Bean, and Rebecca L. Hamilton, "The Role of the Reading Specialist: A Review of Research," *The Reading Teacher*, Vol. 55, No. 3, November 2001, pp. 282–294.

Reback, Randall, "Non-Instructional Spending Improves Non-Cognitive Outcomes: Discontinuity Evidence from a Unique School Counselor Financing System," *Education Finance and Policy*, Vol. 5, No. 2, Spring 2010a, pp. 105–137.

Reback, Randall, "Schools' Mental Health Services and Young Children's Emotions," *Journal of Policy Analysis and Management*, Vol. 29, No. 4, Fall 2010b, pp. 698–725.

Reschly, Daniel, "Learning Disabilities Identification: Primary Intervention, Secondary Intervention, and Then What?" *Journal of Learning Disabilities*, Vol. 38, No. 6, November–December 2005, pp. 510–515.

Roza, Marguerite, Katherine Hagan, and Laura Anderson, "Variation Is the Norm: A Landscape Analysis of Weighted Student Funding Implementation," *Public Budgeting and Finance*, Summer 2020.

Scammacca, Nancy K., Greg Roberts, Sharon Vaughn, and Karla K. Stuebing, "A Meta-Analysis of Interventions for Struggling Readers in Grades 4–12: 1980–2011," *Journal of Learning Disabilities*, Vol. 48, No. 4, July 2015, pp. 369–390.

Slavin, Robert E., Nancy Madden, Margarita Calderón, Anne Chamberlain, and Megan Hennessy, "Reading and Language Outcomes of a Multiyear Randomized Evaluation of Transitional Bilingual Education," *Educational Evaluation and Policy Analysis*, Vol. 33, No. 1, 2011, pp. 47–58.

Swanson, H. Lee., and Maureen Hoskyn, "Experimental Intervention Research on Students with Learning Disabilities: A Meta-Analysis of Treatment Outcomes," *Review of Educational Research*, Vol. 68, No. 3, 1998, pp. 277–321.

Taylor, Rebecca D., Eva Oberle, Joseph A. Durlak, and Roger P. Weissberg, "Promoting Positive Youth Development Through School-Based Social and Emotional Learning Interventions: A Meta-Analysis of Follow-Up Effects," *Child Development*, Vol. 88, No. 4, July 2017, pp. 1156–1171.

Walsh, Mary E., George F. Madaus, Anastasia Raczek, Eric Dearing, Claire Foley, Chen An, Terrence J. Lee-St. John, and Alfred Beaton, "A New Model for Student Support in High-Poverty Urban Elementary Schools Effects on Elementary and Middle School Academic Outcomes," *American Educational Research Journal*, Vol. 51, No. 4, 2014, pp. 704–737.

Wanzek, Jeanne, Elizabeth A. Stevens, Kelly J. Williams, Nancy Scammacca, Sharon Vaughn, and Katherine Sargent, "Current Evidence on the Effects of Intensive Early Reading Interventions," *Journal of Learning Disabilities*, Vol. 51, No. 6, November–December 2018, pp. 612–624.

Wanzek, Jeanne, Sharon Vaughn, Nancy K. Scammacca, Kristina Metz, Christy S. Murray, Greg Roberts, and Louis Danielson, "Extensive Reading Interventions for Students with Reading Difficulties After Grade 3," *Review of Educational Research*, Vol. 83, No. 2, 2013, pp. 163–195.